BUSINESS ETIQUETTE

Better Management Skills

This highly popular range of inexpensive paperbacks covers all areas of basic management. Practical, easy to read and instantly accessible, these guides will help managers to improve their business or communication skills. Those marked * are available on audio cassette.

The books in this series can be tailored to specific company requirements. For further details, please contact the publisher, Kogan Page, telephone 0171-278 0433, fax 0171-837 6348.

Be a Successful Supervisor
Business Etiquette
Business Creativity
Coaching Your Employees
Conducting Effective Interviews
Counselling Your Staff
Creative Decision-making
Creative Thinking in Business
Effective Employee Participation
Effective Meeting Skills
Effective Performance Appraisals*
Effective Presentation Skills
Empowerment
First Time Supervisor
Get Organised!
Goals and Goal Setting
How to Communicate Effectively*

BUSINESS ETIQUETTE

**Your Complete Guide to Correct
Behaviour in Business**

David Robinson

KOGAN
PAGE

First published in 1994
Reprinted 1996, 1997

Kogan Page Limited
120 Pentonville Road
London N1 9JN

© David F Robinson 1994

British Library Cataloguing in Publication Data

A CIP record for this book is available from the British Library.

ISBN 0-7494-1183-X

Typeset by BookEns Ltd, Royston, Herts.
Printed and bound in Great Britain by Clays Ltd, St Ives plc.

Contents

Contents

CHAPTER 1

Introduction

There is an unwritten code of *good business manners* which governs the way that individuals and their companies should deal with each other to:

- Work effectively and profitably together
- Establish and sustain successful long-term relationships
- Improve their own development and promotion potential.

Familiarity with the code gives you the ability to handle demanding business situations with confidence and allows your real talents to be recognised. Not knowing and observing the code doesn't necessarily condemn you to failure – *it just makes being successful more difficult!*

Mastering these rules of business etiquette is not difficult – it just needs a modest investment of study time and the willingness to challenge your own behaviour to see how it can be made more effective. It's like becoming a competent car driver – once achieved you can concentrate on your destination and not worry all the time that you'll crash the gears!

Good business manners are, in essence, the commercial application of acceptable personal behaviour. There can be no excuse for acting with perfect gentility in private life and like Genghis Khan in business! We all know, however, that what might be acceptable in one context might be quite wrong in another. So it is in business. Hence the need to beware the assumption that every rule of personal manners translates directly into its business equivalent.

This book gives you *a simple and practical guide* to handling business situations, both common and uncommon, in which you will be expected to show your command of correct behaviour. However highly you may rate your manners, it will be surprising if you don't find major ways in which you can improve as a result of reading the text and completing the questionnaires and checklists.

When all else is equal, the person who behaves better will win. In that sense, being well-mannered is a real, if surprising, source of personal and corporate competitive advantage. Spending time on achieving it must represent a good investment.

About the text

In each chapter we explore a different aspect of your business relationships and the challenges that you are likely to meet. The process starts with dealing with people face to face and progresses through to more complex situations, such as handling meetings. Principles established in earlier chapters are not generally repeated later in the text, and so it is important to read the chapters in the right order. Once read, of course, you may wish to use the text for reference on particular points of difficulty.

This book is aimed at the business person – irrespective of sex. Good business manners should be universal and neither sex should claim special privileges or have special obligations. When you find references to 'he', 'him' or 'his' in the text, the male pronoun has been used for simplicity and the female pronoun could just as readily be substituted.

Finally, you should remember that, although *the basic principles are timeless*, the subject of what constitutes good manners is one which is always developing, as attitudes and habits change. You should always be alert to those changes and regard any book on the subject, including this one, as the foundation on which to build a better understanding of them.

CHAPTER 2
The Golden Rules of Good Business Manners

The underlying principle of good business manners is *the thoughtful consideration of the interests and feelings of others.* In other words, you must show by what you do and say that you care as much about the person you are dealing with as for yourself. This doesn't mean that you shouldn't be tough when it's needed or unbusinesslike – nobody likes or respects the smarmy and ingratiating individual who butters up his colleagues and business associates. Rather it is showing from the way you conduct yourself that you have well-founded personal values, based on respect for others, which permeate everything you do. So if you have to settle an argument, discipline a subordinate or sack someone, your manner will be not only firm and fair but sympathetic to their personal circumstances.

In many cases it takes a real effort of will to overcome your natural instinct to take advantage of someone in a weaker position. By doing so you will not only win the respect of others but also enhance your own confidence and self-esteem. Thinking of the other person's point of view before you act has many such valuable benefits!

The golden rules

Showing that you care for the feelings of others in the way that you behave in business can be encapsulated in the word 'IMPACT' which summarises the golden rules:

I	ntegrity	act in an honest and truthful way
M	anners	never be selfish, boorish or undisciplined
P	ersonality	communicate your own values, attitudes and opinions
A	ppearance	always present yourself to best advantage
C	onsideration	see yourself from the other person's standpoint
T	act	think before you speak.

Integrity is the demonstration by what you do and say that you are an honest, truthful and trustworthy person. A reputation for integrity is slowly gained but quickly lost. Much business would grind to a halt if there wasn't a basic, positive assumption about people's integrity. It is tested when the individual or his company is provoked or tempted to act less than honestly. It is a golden rule of good business behaviour that your integrity should be unquestioned – no amount of camouflage can disguise its lack.

Manners are the patterns of behaviour which indicate to the person you are dealing with whether you can be relied on to act correctly and fairly when he does business with you. If he thinks that you are boorish, selfish or undisciplined, your relationship is unlikely to prosper. Equally, if you speak or act in a racist or sexist way, or show disloyalty to your company or colleagues, your manners will be seen as unacceptable. Avoiding the negative is only half the story. Good manners involve taking positive action to make the other person feel good about your relationship with him. Much of this book is concerned with this golden rule.

Your own **Personality** is what you can uniquely offer the business you work in. You should aim to ensure that the way you behave gives the best possible opportunity for your qualities to be appreciated. For example, you can be passionate about business but shouldn't be emotional; you can be irreverent but not disloyal; you can be amusing but not flippant and you can be brilliant but not boring. Don't let lack of consideration for others, thoughtless or tactless actions or a failure to observe the civilities of business life mark you down as being beyond the pale.

Your **Appearance** may not be your most valuable asset, but it should never be a liability! Being well-groomed, wearing appropriate clothes, standing and sitting in a good posture and taking care of yourself physically, are all vital elements in making and sustaining a good impression on your business colleagues. We all react, if only subconsciously, to the way people we deal with look. Don't let your appearance let you down!

Consideration for others is the fundamental principle underlying all good manners in business. Successful negotiators often role play the likely actions of their opposite numbers before meeting them. The objective is simple – to be ready to respond to new initiatives when they occur. In the same way the business person who has imagined, in advance, the potential reaction of the person he is to meet, write to or speak to on the telephone, is immediately able to deal with them with more care and sensitivity.

Tact is the last, but not the least, of the golden rules because it should be the 'Gatekeeper', protecting us from thoughtless words and actions. Everyone in business knows the temptation to react immediately to some provocation or to take some perceived advantage, and the regret which follows if we act on impulse. Tact is not just about putting unpleasant matters in an acceptable way. It involves careful thought for the interests of others and only then choosing the most acceptable form of expression. The subtext of this golden rule is that when in doubt you should say nothing!

What is your IMPACT rating?

The self-assessment test which follows is for your eyes only. Answer the questions truthfully and see how far your business behaviour matches up to what it should be. Check your score against the rating shown on pages 17–18.
5 = best, 1 = worst answer.

Business Etiquette

	Always	Sometimes	Never

1. Your integrity

(a) Once I've given my word I can be relied on to keep it.

(b) I tell white lies to avoid embarrassing other people.

(c) I reclaim a little bit more on my expenses than I've actually spent.

(d) When under pressure I'm prepared to bend the rules for the benefit of my company.

(e) My business colleagues think highly of my integrity.

2. Your business manners

(a) I am courteous and considerate when dealing with the opposite sex.

(b) I try to be polite however much I dislike or am irritated by the other person.

(c) I enjoy gossip, particularly when it's about my colleagues.

(d) I'm loyal to my company, even when I think they're in the wrong.

(e) I impose my authority on my juniors by whatever means appear most effective at the time.

3. Your personality and style

(a) I believe that humour is a vital part of getting on well with people.

(b) I like to tell my colleagues about my home life and interests.

	Always	Sometimes	Never

(c) Colleagues should share their opinions on contentious issues such as politics, religion and sex.

(d) I make sure that my views and attitudes mean that I stand out from the crowd.

(e) I am liked and respected by my colleagues.

4. Your appearance

(a) I dress in a way that suits me, not for the benefit of other people.

(b) I take as much care over my appearance when I'm among colleagues as I do when I'm meeting people from outside the business.

(c) How well I do my job is more important to me than how I look when doing it.

(d) I compare how I look with the best turned-out of my colleagues.

(e) I judge other people on how they dress and on their grooming.

5. How considerate are you?

(a) I think about the feelings of others and adapt my own actions accordingly.

(b) Life in business is so competitive that I take any advantage I am offered.

Business Etiquette

	Always	Sometimes	Never

(c) I recognise and remember favours done to me and repay them when I can.

(d) I enjoy listening to the other person's views before expressing my own.

(e) When I'm in a hurry I see nothing wrong in cutting the other person short, however rude it may seem at the time.

6. How tactful are you?

(a) I try to break bad news to people in a sympathetic way.

(b) I don't mind interrupting someone if I think the subject is sufficiently important.

(c) I keep to myself personal information about my colleagues which might be harmful to them in either their business or private lives.

(d) I am prepared to sit quietly while a senior says something foolish in front of people from outside the business.

(e) I do not remind people of previous mistakes they have made or problems they have encountered.

Checklist scores

		Always	Sometimes	Never
1.	**Your integrity**			
	(a)	5	3	1
	(b)	3	5	1
	(c)	1	3	5
	(d)	1	3	5
	(e)	5	3	1
2.	**Your business manners**			
	(a)	5	3	1
	(b)	5	3	1
	(c)	1	5	3
	(d)	5	3	1
	(e)	1	3	5
3.	**Your personality and style**			
	(a)	3	5	1
	(b)	3	5	1
	(c)	1	5	3
	(d)	3	5	1
	(e)	5	3	1
4.	**Your appearance**			
	(a)	1	5	3
	(b)	5	3	1
	(c)	1	5	3
	(d)	5	3	1
	(e)	3	5	1

5. **How considerate are you?**

(a)	3	5	1
(b)	1	3	5
(c)	5	3	1
(d)	5	3	1
(e)	1	3	5

6. **How tactful are you?**

(a)	5	3	1
(b)	1	5	3
(c)	5	3	1
(d)	3	5	1
(e)	5	3	1

If you scored:

120–150 You're among the most considerate business people around. You should have nothing to worry about but maybe the rest of the book will refresh some of those parts that day-to-day experiences don't reach.

80–120 You're doing fairly well but there are aspects of your behaviour which could do with improvement. Don't accept second best – see whether you can join the premier league.

50–80 You have problems with business manners and need to do something urgent about the way you behave. Now read on!

30–50 You can't score fewer than 30 and so if you're in this band you're either not scoring yourself seriously or you haven't got the point of it all. Why not reread the chapter and have another go?

CHAPTER 3
Dealing with People Face to Face

The most important demonstration of your command of good business manners is when you deal with people face to face. They are able to assess the whole person – your dress, your posture, your facial expression and your speech – in a way which is impossible when speaking on the telephone or dealing with you in writing.

You should never need to be on your best behaviour but always able easily and confidently to adopt the most appropriate manner for the person (or people) you are dealing with at that moment. If you are always at your ease, knowing exactly how to conduct yourself, their confidence and regard for you will be immeasurably increased. In this chapter we examine the *rules of good manners* applying to the most common face-to-face occasions which occur in business.

Meeting for the first time

Before you arrive
Dress appropriately for the occasion. Possibilities range from 'smart formal' (business suit and the female equivalent) for most businesses to 'smart informal' (well-tailored shirts, trousers and jackets for men and informal wear for women) for creative, media and similar businesses. When in doubt, always dress more formally than might be appropriate. Your clothes should

be well pressed and your shoes clean. Let your clothes express your personality but remember that you are dressed to make the person you are meeting feel comfortable – not just for yourself.

Find out what you can about *the person you are meeting*, in particular about any strong views or interests he has. Knowing which subjects are likely to prove acceptable (and unacceptable) in conversation is an invaluable aid to an effective meeting. This need for preparation extends, of course, to the subject of your meeting and any relevant background. It is bad manners to arrive at a prearranged meeting ill prepared. It not only wastes the time of the person you are meeting but also gives a very poor impression of you and your company.

In reception

Arrive in good time for your appointment. Be polite to the receptionist (always smile and say 'Good morning') and be patient if they are busy when you arrive. Give your name and the name of the person you are visiting and make it clear that you have an appointment. If you are more than ten minutes early for your meeting, suggest to the receptionist that she doesn't immediately announce your arrival. (Some people find it embarrassing to keep visitors waiting in reception areas for more than a few minutes and your early arrival may be inconvenient for them.)

The receptionist should offer you refreshment if you have to wait but don't take your cup in with you when shown to your host's office (if for no other reason than that it's difficult to shake hands with a briefcase in one hand and a coffee cup in the other!). A visit to the toilet before your meeting will also give you an opportunity to make sure that your hair is well brushed, tie neatly knotted and so on.

If the receptionist is not too busy, pleasant conversation will often yield useful information about your host's business that you can refer to during your meeting. When being shown to your host's office by the receptionist or secretary it is polite to exchange some appropriate pleasantries (the weather, how long she has worked for the company and holidays are good standbys) to avoid an uncomfortable hiatus between the reception area and the office.

If you are unfamiliar with the office, it is perfectly good manners for a female receptionist or secretary to precede a male visitor through doors and into lifts. It is usual for the receptionist or secretary to announce you when showing you into the host's office. If they don't say your name, do so yourself immediately you enter the room.

Introductions

It is courteous for your host (whether male or female) to rise to greet you whatever your relative seniority. Other male colleagues in the room should also rise although female colleagues commonly remain seated. A *handshake* is the universally recognised form of greeting (delivered firmly but not bone-crushingly, with *a smile* and full *eye contact*) and should be simultaneously offered by your host and you. You should greet every other person in the room in the same way, in turn, as the host introduces them to you. If the host or his colleagues fails to offer you the customary handshake, you should not press the point beyond the initial gesture.

Don't sit down until your host invites you to – if he fails to offer you a seat, ask politely if it is in order for you to sit down. This courtesy should be observed even if you are much more senior than the person you are visiting. Some male hosts assist female visitors to be seated but the practice is rapidly dying out (other than at dinner parties) since many females find it (quite understandably) rather patronising.

It is the duty of the host to *introduce to you any colleagues* he has with him (and vice versa if you are accompanied by a more junior colleague), giving not only their names but also their job titles and any other relevant information. It is his task to make you feel at ease and it is good manners to offer you refreshment at the beginning of the meeting irrespective of the time of day. It is usual to accept the offer but there is nothing wrong in declining politely.

Business cards

Whether or not you offer your business card at the beginning of a meeting requires careful thought although you should always respond if your host opens the meeting by offering his own. If the two organisations that you both represent are well known to each other, even though you haven't met your host before, offering your card is probably best left to the end of the meeting when, for example, follow-up action is being discussed. If your host is unfamiliar with your company or you wish to establish your personal credentials or seniority, offering your card at the beginning of the meeting is good practice. Exchanging cards interrupts the flow of a meeting, not least because people will want to read them rather than talk, and so it is better, if in doubt, to leave them until the end.

Familiarity

If more than one person is involved on either side, the more senior normally takes the lead, inviting the junior colleague to contribute as needed, at least until the ice is broken. You should always start by adopting *a formal style of address* such as 'Mr Jones' (or 'Sir' if you feel the other person's seniority requires it – but remember that some people find being addressed in that way irritatingly obsequious) and wait to be invited to use first names. Even if your more senior colleague is put on these terms, do not assume that it also applies to you until that is made clear. If you are the more senior person, remember to draw your junior colleague into the conversation whenever relevant and to treat him with appropriate good manners. Never address your remarks solely to one person if several are involved, but make sure that you establish full eye contact with each person from time to time (it is through this type of contact that people subconsciously assess truthfulness and integrity).

Don't remove your jacket or loosen your tie unless your host has already done so or invites you to do so. If you would feel more comfortable in shirtsleeves, politely ask your host's permission, making sure that your jacket isn't half way off when you do so (making it embarrassing for him to say 'No'). In very hot conditions you look smarter without a tie than with one half way down your shirt front.

Familiarity and ease of conversation spring naturally from *mutual confidence*, which is itself based on clarity of thought and speech, and attentive listening. You should show that you are alert and interested in what your host has to say, watch for clues about the things which he values and respond briefly and intelligently when needed. If you clearly identify with *his* interests and concerns, you should find that a comfortable familiarity quickly follows.

It is both good business and good manners to *control your emotions* during face-to-face meetings avoiding extremes of anger, disappointment or frustration. Keeping cool whatever the provocation is an admirable virtue and you should never forget your business manners even if the meeting proves to be a disaster from start to finish.

Down to business

At most first meetings the two parties want to size up what sort of person the other is before getting down to business. This is best done by using some neutral topic introduced by you or your host when you first meet. You might, for example, talk about your journey to the meeting or refer to an acquaintance who used to work for your host's company or admire the offices or its products – the possibilities are limitless. You should always make your comments interesting, brief, uncontentious and offering an opportunity for your host to respond. Never use this 'getting to know you' period to blow your own trumpet.

If your host prefers to get down to business right away, you should do likewise. Don't offer personal anecdotes or snaps of the family unless invited to. Remember that your host probably has many other calls on his time. If you are the host, it is courteous to indicate to your visitor at the beginning of a meeting the time of your next commitment. This ensures that you don't end up with an embarrassing phase of clock-watching as you overrun or have to cram three-quarters of the subject matter into the last five minutes.

Smoking

Smoking is almost universally regarded nowadays as *antisocial behaviour* in offices and should only be practised at the explicit invitation of your host. Asking, 'Do you mind if I smoke?' will almost always be met with, 'Of course not', out of politeness (the scurrying around to find an ashtray will normally indicate how uncommon an activity it has become) but the damage is done the moment you light up. Your behaviour will have been classified as bad mannered. Even if your host is a smoker, it is polite not to smoke if other non-smokers are present.

Taking notes

You should always *ask the permission of your host* before taking notes during a meeting. You should not plonk your pad on the desk at the beginning of a meeting (or invade the privacy of your host's desk space with any other of your impedimenta) but wait until you have his permission to take notes. Tape recording a conversation is almost guaranteed to make it artificial and to kill any spontaneity – it should only be requested in the rare circumstances when a verbatim record is needed.

Taking your leave

At the end of a meeting it is important to repeat the courtesies which introduced it. The handshake, smile and eye contact should all cement a relationship which has developed during your discussion. If your host remembers you by the consideration you showed for him and his needs and the easy and pleasant way that you conducted yourself, you should be assured of his future *good opinion*. If you thought too much of yourself and ignored his conventions, you can expect a less flattering result.

The job interview

There are *special conventions* which apply only to the job interview. This is because the interviewer is assessing all aspects of the candidate's suitability for the post – including his business manners – and there are usually no second chances if the applicant gets things wrong.

The secret of being a *successful interviewee* is to eliminate any danger that you will be rejected simply because you have failed to follow the rules of good business behaviour. Of course, this won't guarantee that you'll get the job! Simply that you'll be judged on your merits.

Your curriculum vitae

Before getting to the interview stage you will probably have to submit a CV. Many good applicants are rejected because they fail to impress the reader with the content or presentation of their CV. If you follow these simple principles you shouldn't go far wrong:

- *Type* both the CV and the short covering letter that should go with it (some employers insist on handwritten applications – if they do, make sure that your writing is as legible as possible).
- Keep your CV to no more than *two pages* (remember that the recruiter will probably have to read dozens of applications).
- Start with *personal information* (your name, address, sex, marital status, age and so on) followed by a summary of your *academic achievements* (give dates and grades of exams passed).
- Expand on your *current job*, giving details of your remuneration package and reasons for looking to change jobs.
- Give a brief account of *previous jobs* (in chronological order) giving the last salary and the reason for leaving.
- Summarise your *leisure* and other out-of-work interests.
- Close with a couple of lines on *why the particular opportunity is attractive to you*.

References are usually not needed before the interview stage and you should think carefully before attaching letters of commendation to your CV. The job history you set out in the CV should be sufficiently persuasive without the need for extra evidence at this stage.

At the interview

All the normal rules of smart appearance, early arrival and pre-meeting preparation apply to the job interview. However, the interview is special because you will probably have a very limited time to make a good impression – and you will have no idea in advance how the interviewer will want to conduct the meeting. The answer is to prepare for the following possibilities:

- You will be asked to *describe your career*. Rehearse a brief and interesting summary giving most emphasis to your most recent or current job, highlighting experience particularly relevant to the post in question and lasting no more than ten minutes (assuming no questions are asked in the meantime).
- You will be asked to explain *why this job appeals* to you and why you are suitable for it – more difficult to prepare because you will have less to go on (and if necessary you should say this to the interviewer) but as a minimum you should have the 'headlines' clearly fixed in your mind.
- You will be asked *technical or personal questions* apparently at random and perhaps in an aggressive way to test your speed of thought and resilience. Be prepared to have to think on your feet, don't lose your cool and, above all, don't attempt miracles (the interviewer may be testing the maturity of your reaction to unfairly difficult questions).

In the first 30 seconds of the interview your appearance, manner and personal style will be assessed by the interviewer – either favourably or otherwise. It is vital that you appear *confident, alert and cheerful* (smile, even if you are feeling extremely nervous). Greeting, shaking hands, eye contact and good posture (whether standing or sitting) all play an essential part. Your interviewer may be tired, bad-tempered, poorly organised ('What did you say your name was again?') or someone you instantly dislike. You must carry on regardless – if only to feel afterwards that at least you did yourself justice!

Talking about yourself
Don't be shy about speaking of your achievements but don't exaggerate them or be too self-congratulatory. For example, it is better to say, 'I was lucky enough to lead the warehouse computerisation project' than 'The MD chose me as obviously the best person to lead the warehouse computerisation project which was a brilliant success'.

Resist the temptation to 'massage' the facts in your favour – for example, the importance of your previous jobs or the salary that you earned. Experienced recruiters can quickly spot the inconsistencies of these fictions and most facts can be quickly checked anyway.

If you feel the interviewer is not giving you the opportunity to bring out a particular feature of your skills or background, you should politely take the initiative at a suitable break in the discussion.

Answering questions
The interviewer will both want to ask you questions and expect you to have questions for him about the vacant post. His questions usually come first and the way you answer is often as important as what you say.

The golden rules of responding to questions are:

- Don't be either obsequious ('that's an extremely good question, if I may say so, Sir') or too flippant ('Cor, that's a cracking question') but *react seriously and naturally*.
- *Answer the question* that is asked and not the question which you would have preferred to have been asked (this involves listening carefully to what is said to you).
- Keep the answer *brief and relevant* – it is better to ask the interviewer if he would like more detail than to launch into a lengthy and unwanted diatribe.
- If you don't know the answer (for example, to a technical question) say so immediately – *don't try to bluff* your way out of it.

Don't be afraid to be humorous but avoid telling jokes which are not usually relevant to an interview situation.

When asking questions, avoid the interrogation trap which suggests that you distrust what you have been told or are trying to outwit your interviewer. You should aim to get the information you need in as effective and pleasant a way as you can without irritating the interviewer. If you have no questions say so, but thank the interviewer for the opportunity to ask.

Winding up
The smile, handshake and eye contact are as essential at the end of the interview as at the beginning. You should not hesitate to ask the interviewer what will be the next stage in the process (if he has not already explained that to you) and it is perfectly correct for you to assure him of your continued interest in the post. It is important that you leave the interviewer with a positive impression and so you should never close by expressing a worry, a personal problem or scepticism about the job being for you.

Assess your own performance (1)

Complete the following questionnaire, by circling your answer, and compare your understanding of the rules of good behaviour discussed so far in this chapter with the answers on pages 39–40.

1. You've been asked to meet a new business contact at his office an hour's cross-country drive away from yours. How long do you leave for the journey: (a) an hour; (b) an hour and a half; or (c) two hours?
2. Your host keeps you waiting for 40 minutes in reception and you are running short of time before your next meeting. Do you: (a) suggest you rearrange the meeting for another day; (b) try to put back your next appointment; or (c) start the meeting and suggest a continuation meeting on another day?

3. If you arrive at a meeting and your host tells you he expected someone more senior than you to deal with him, do you: (a) suggest you make an appointment for your boss and then leave; (b) suggest that you take the meeting as far as possible and refer any difficult matters to your boss later; or (c) try to persuade your host that you are the right person to handle his business?

4. You find that your host has several colleagues with him whom he doesn't introduce. Should you: (a) ask for introductions straight away; (b) wait for them to speak and ask them who they are then; or (c) try to work out who they are as you go along and ask for confirmation at the end of the meeting?

5. During a meeting your host asks you questions which you regard as being too personal and would prefer not to answer. Do you: (a) tell him politely to mind his own business; (b) reply in a jokey and non-committal manner; or (c) answer the questions but politely explain your reservations about doing so?

6. Your host speaks extremely quickly and rather indistinctly with the result that you are liable to miss some crucial pieces of information during the meeting. Do you: (a) ask him to repeat everything slowly and clearly; (b) suggest that he prepares a written note after the meeting confirming the key points; or (c) struggle on making the best sense you can of what you hear?

7. On the way to a meeting you find that your best suit has lost a button and that your tie acquired a large soup stain during lunch. Do you: (a) keep your jacket on and your hand over the missing button; (b) mention these setbacks with a joke at the beginning of the meeting; or (c) carry on regardless?

8. When about to shake hands with your host you find that he has an artificial right arm. Do you: (a) offer your left hand in greeting; (b) abandon the attempt to shake hands; or (c) wait for your host to respond to your approach?

9. At a recruitment interview your interviewer seems uninterested in the aspect of your career which you think

is most relevant. Should you: (a) ask him why he appears to be ignoring it; (b) press ahead to tell him about it at the next suitable point in the interview; or (c) assume that the interviewer knows best and leave it to him?

10. Your interviewer asks you to tell him what you consider to be your worst fault. Do you: (a) assume it's a trick question and answer 'not suffering fools gladly' or some such self-congratulatory phrase; (b) answer genuinely but with some mitigating comments; or (c) sidestep the question?

11. It's clear from the beginning that you and your interviewer are not going to see eye to eye. Should you: (a) cut the interview short by offering to leave; (b) ask to be seen by someone else; or (c) carry on regardless?

12. You find that you have been caught out in 'improving' the status and salary of your last job. Should you: (a) try to give a plausible explanation; (b) apologise and explain the reason for the lapse; or (c) cut and run?

13. The more you hear about the job you're being interviewed for the less you like the sound of it. Do you: (a) wait for the end of the interview and explain your views then; (b) keep quiet and regard the interview as good practice; or (c) express your reservations to the interviewer straight away and leave the meeting?

14. You are being interviewed by a panel and have stage fright in front of so many people. Should you: (a) look at one individual and pretend that it's a one-to-one interview; (b) explain that you are very nervous and ask for their consideration; or (c) struggle on wishing you were somewhere completely different?

15. Although you have already been offered a job by one firm, you have not accepted it until you have seen whether the post available with another looks more attractive. At the end of the interview with the second firm their job seems better and you have to decide whether to: (a) tell them that you have another offer to improve your chances of a quick decision; (b) keep quiet and hope that their offer will come

through before you have to make a decision on the first; or (c) explain that you would like a decision by a particular date without saying why?

Customers, suppliers and colleagues

Although the same basic rules of good manners apply to all your face-to-face dealings with others, there are additional points you need to look out for when dealing with these three categories of people.

Who has the initiative?
If you are dealing with a *customer*, your job is to facilitate communication whether he is making an enquiry, placing an order or making a complaint. You must take the initiative in expressing your willingness to help – and then stop talking and *listen*! Too many sales people make assumptions about what the customer needs and go off into a completely ineffective sales patter. It is both irritating and inefficient. When you are clear what the customer wants, you should be polite and businesslike – finishing off the conversation with a clear statement of what happens next; for example, 'I'll put your order in hand today and you can expect delivery before next Tuesday. Thank you very much'.

If you are dealing with a *supplier* you should either know before the meeting what you want or be clear what features you are looking for in the product or service being offered. Salesmen like to deal with clear-thinking buyers who often end up by getting a better price! It is up to you, as the buyer, to take the initiative in the discussion, making sure that you politely but firmly keep the salesman to the subject *you* want to discuss and not what *he* would prefer to sell you!

When dealing with *colleagues* it is important to remember that, if it is you who called the meeting or made the first approach (by, for example, visiting a colleague's office), you owe it to them to say:

- *Why* you want to speak to them
- How urgent the *problem* is
- What are the *facts*.

If the other person is more senior than you, don't be surprised or offended if he decides that the matter can be dealt with at a different time or in a different way. After all, he will have other priorities and calls on his time. If the person is more junior, he has little option but to listen to you, if only out of respect. It is therefore doubly important that you don't waste his time.

Judging seniority

When dealing with people from outside your own organisation it can be difficult to know how senior they are. *Look for clues* in appearance, self-confidence, knowledge of the subject and apparent authority to commit their company. You are unlikely to come across many eccentric multi-millionaires who dress and behave like floor-sweepers and you will soon build experience of what you can expect of typical levels of manager. The simplest thing, of course, is to ask – but if you do, make sure that you do so tactfully and at an appropriate moment in the conversation. For example, it is better when asking the question to suggest that the person is *more* senior than they are likely to be than *less*. Most importantly, you should not adopt an informal style until you are sure that it will be acceptable to the other person, given your relative seniorities.

Making face-to-face discussions effective

Most people find that the better they know another person they deal with in business, the more effective they can make their face-to-face discussions. We get to know how formal or informal the other person likes to be, what blend of social and business content is best in the meeting and whether there are any idiosyncracies, prejudices or special 'no go' areas of conversation.

If you are dealing with someone *for the first time,* none of this understanding has been developed and the best you can hope for is to create a strong businesslike impression on which to build. The essential ingredients of this are as follows:

- *Prepare* yourself before the discussion takes place – know what you want to cover and what outcome you are aiming for. If possible, find out from colleagues or contacts something about the person you will be dealing with and adapt your conversation accordingly.
- Be ready to *get quickly to the point* of the discussion and to follow through with a focused exchange – leave the 'by the way' observations to the end of the meeting.
- Make a *short record there and then* of matters decided during the conversation to avoid later misunderstanding and the risk of remembering incorrectly. It is good practice to close a discussion with an oral résumé, for example, 'Fine, Mr Baxter. You'll get those production figures to me by Friday and I'll let you have our firm price quotation by Monday afternoon.'

Handling conflict

When conflict arises, participants often 'lose their cool' with the result that rational discussion is replaced with emotional mudslinging. You can, of course, feel rightly passionate about an issue and communicating this in a business discussion is one of the weapons of effective persuasion. If you lose your self-control, however, you are almost certain to become irrational and many relationships are irreparably damaged by things said in this state of mind. Some intentionally use aggressive and unsettling techniques in order to gain an advantage over the other person. It is up to you to make sure that they don't succeed!

You should act as follows:

- Watch for the conflict *warning signs*. There will be an unexpected formality (the other person might start calling you 'Mr Watkins' instead of the usual 'Jim'); he may call one or more colleagues to join what would normally be a one-to-one discussion; he may start to go red in the face, become less coherent in speech and avoid eye contact.

- Observe the other person's behaviour very acutely and *think through carefully any answers* you give or observations you make. If the other person starts to raise the temperature (for example, by shouting or swearing) be progressively quieter and more deliberate in what you say.
- Don't get drawn into a *shouting match*. If matters get to a point where you think it best to leave, do so quickly and politely (you might say, for example, 'I'm sorry you feel so strongly about this, George. I suggest we meet again in a few days' time when we've both had time to reflect on this conversation').
- *Ignore personal abuse.* Remember that the argument is most likely to be between two companies – not two individuals.
- *Enlist the help of colleagues* to resolve serious conflict – don't struggle on on your own and get thoroughly out of your depth.

Respecting confidences

If you are going to give someone information which you want treated in confidence, say so *before* you give the information to allow the other person to assess whether receiving it will put them in a difficult or embarrassing position. If you are likely to be put in that position, tell the other person immediately and let them judge the importance and relevance of what they have to say. It is often impossible to accept as confidential information which might be of value to your business, and it is better to make this clear at the time than to appear to be untrustworthy when you pass it on to your colleagues later. We all make the occasional error of letting slip information which was given to us in confidence. The best we can do is to trust that these lapses will be treated as such – and not as being habitual.

Keeping colleagues informed

There is a balance to be struck between telling everyone everything that is going on and being secretive. Good business behaviour is about thinking through what is relevant and useful to other people's interests and then taking appropriate action. Thus, you should always report on personal meetings which impact on the work of your colleagues either orally (particularly when they may want to discuss the implications of what you have to say) or by memo (when the outcome is 'for information'). There is a lot to be said for brief, handwritten notes which can be photocopied and circulated without taking up secretarial time.

Building relationships

People gain confidence in you when you deal fairly and effectively with them over a period. Personal liking and respect follow caring concern for each other's interests and the test of such relationships is how quickly and easily problems can be sorted out when things go wrong. At an appropriate stage *business colleagues become friends* and such friendships often survive job changes and retirement.

The key to building successful relationships is to find the right mix between being businesslike and being friendly. It is important to know the people you regularly deal with as individuals, and business entertaining and social events have an important part to play in this wider dimension. You should also keep an eye open for things which might be interesting to them (such as business opportunities for their firm) whether or not it will help your company. Take an interest in their family and remember to congratulate them if they receive awards or are promoted. Always speak well of business contacts you value – much as you would hope they speak well of you.

It is equally important to build successful *relationships with your colleagues* in your own firm. This entails consideration for them, as individuals, and not relying on your seniority to carry you through the day. The most successful managers show a caring attitude to all their staff and an ability to be courteous and understanding, whatever the pressures. We have all come across managers who dump work and problems on subordinates without thought. They are not people who build successful relationships – just reputations for being dreadful to work for!

Dealing with your boss

Your future promotion will, in part, depend on the way that you deal with your boss, both in the day-to-day context of your job and when you have more formal review discussions. There are some important principles of good business behaviour to be observed if this relationship is to be successful from both party's point of view:

- However informal the relationship may be, you should never forget that your boss has responsibilities within the *company hierarchy* which he must observe. Don't put him in embarrassing or unfair positions (for example, by asking him to comment on personalities or on his superiors) and support his decisions even though you may have strong reservations about them.
- *Be loyal* to him and to your colleagues. Don't allow yourself to be drawn into criticising your peers or retailing office gossip, and defend your boss from criticism when necessary; equally, you should give your subordinates the benefit of the doubt and be prepared to take personal responsibility for their mistakes.
- If you have *complaints* which concern your boss, address them, in confidence, to him in a reasoned (and reasonable) way – don't use the grapevine or coded signals to make your point.
- If you are dissatisfied with the way your boss has dealt with an issue, you should only refer the matter to *a more senior*

person with his knowledge and with a sufficient period of notice to allow him to reconsider. You should *never* go over your boss's head for a decision or report a concern without following this routine.

- You should adopt a *style of personal behaviour* which ensures that you fit in with the team in which you work. This doesn't mean that you have to become faceless; simply make sure that your talents and efforts are not obscured from your colleagues and your boss by differences of style (for example, of dress, time-keeping, language or habits of socialising with colleagues).

No one can guarantee that their boss will fully appreciate their potential. What you can and should do is make sure that your behaviour in the workplace is as thoughtful and considerate to your colleagues as it is to the third parties with whom you normally deal.

Assess your own performance (2)

Complete the following questionnaire, by circling your answer, and compare your understanding of the rules of good business behaviour discussed in the last two sections of this chapter with the answers on pages 40–41.

1. You have a charming colleague who will insist on interrupting you at busy times to talk about stamp-collecting. You don't want to upset him but need to get on with more urgent tasks. Should you: (a) drop hints and hope that he catches on; (b) tell him politely that you don't have the time to talk but will happily see him later; or (c) ignore him and carry on with your work?
2. You have called a meeting with a supplier to place an order you have already cleared with your colleagues. When he arrives, however, your boss joins the meeting and starts questioning the need for the work to be carried out and the supplier's ability to do it. Should you: (a) sit back and

let the supplier battle it out; (b) take your colleague to one side and say that he is out of order; or (c) abandon the meeting, with an apology to the supplier, until you and your team are better prepared?

3. You attend a meeting with a customer and find him drunk and abusive. Do you: (a) draw attention to his state and express your distaste for it before leaving; (b) try to humour him and leave on good terms; or (c) invent some excuse and leave immediately?

4. You accidently discover that two colleagues, both married, are having an affair. Do you: (a) take no action and hope that the situation resolves itself; (b) report the affair to your boss and leave it to him to take any action that's needed; or (c) confront the individuals and try to persuade them to cool it?

5. You are told that your company intends to stop using a supplier with whom you have an established and friendly personal relationship. You know that this will have a serious effect on his business and you have to decide whether to: (a) do nothing but prepare yourself to explain the action when he is notified; (b) try to persuade your colleagues to allow you to give the supplier early warning of the decision; or (c) tell the supplier on a personal and confidential basis. Which should you do?

6. A colleague handles a business contact rudely in a meeting that you attend and refuses to apologise afterwards. You feel that your own manners are open to criticism as a result. Should you: (a) apologise to the contact on behalf of your colleague; (b) ask your colleague's boss to make him apologise; or (c) make a friendly call to your contact to make sure that he knows that you are not as boorish as your colleague?

7. You learn that a good customer is being investigated on a charge of shoplifting. When you next speak to him, should you: (a) mention that you know about it and express your best wishes; (b) wait for him to mention it; or (c) reaffirm

your support for him without referring to the specific case?

8. A meeting with an aggrieved customer degenerates to the point that he threatens physical violence. Should you: (a) reciprocate the threat; (b) warn him of the gravity of his threat and call for witnesses; or (c) leave as quickly as possible?

9. You attend a meeting with your boss at which he consistently gets facts wrong and draws incorrect conclusions from them. Is it better for you to: (a) let it go but have a word with him afterwards; (b) politely interrupt to set matters right; or (c) find an excuse to take your colleague to one side to point out his mistakes?

10. You find that a company you have joined expects staff to socialise out of office hours. You are a shy person and have to decide whether to: (a) pretend to be more sociable than you are; (b) do the minimum to keep up appearances; or (c) avoid joining in?

Suggested answers to assessment tests

Assess your own performance (1)
A preferred answer is suggested for each question with a brief explanation.

1. (b) An hour and a half should cover most eventualities. Leaving earlier is probably not a good use of your time.
2. (b) is best if it will not inconvenience your next contact. (c) ensures that you don't embarrass your host for keeping you waiting.
3. (b) must be worth a try but you must be prepared to revert to (a) as soon as things get difficult.
4. (a) is the correct approach so long as you ask in a pleasant way before the discussion starts.
5. (c) is the least evasive or offensive but is never easy to pull off.

6. (a) must be best but you will need to choose your words with care. It is better to attribute the problem to some weakness of your own than to blame the speaker!

7. (c) is the most sensible approach, hoping that your personal behaviour will more than counteract any bad impression made by your less than perfect appearance.

8. (c) react naturally and good humouredly – this situation will have happened dozens of times to your host and he will know best how to handle it.

9. (b) an interview is a dialogue and if you want to introduce a topic you should have the confidence to do so.

10. (b) is the challenging and correct answer – experienced interviewers have heard all the bluffs many times before.

11. (c) is correct since adopting (b) offers little prospect of having a better hearing after your first interviewer has passed on his comments about you.

12. (b) involves eating humble pie but should win a more sympathetic reception than either of the other possibilities.

13. (c) is considerate of the interviewer's time as long as you express your reasons in a clear and helpful way.

14. (a) is the technique that works best for many people and is used by many actors who suffer from the same problem.

15. (c) is the best initial approach which you should be prepared to expand to (a) if pressed. If you are a strong candidate, the prospective employer will be very upset if he doesn't have a fair chance to offer you the post.

Assess your own performance (2)

1. (a) is the polite way to start but move on to (b) if that proves ineffective. (c) is bad-mannered.

2. (b) will save the time and trouble of reconvening a meeting but, if your colleague persists in his objections, revert to (c).

3. (c) is by far the most diplomatic and practical course. If necessary, feign sudden stomach pains – but not as the result of excess alcohol!

4. (a) is best unless you fear that the business might be compromised in some way in which case you should adopt (b).
5. (c) is a considerate and thoughtful course as long as your contact will respect the confidence absolutely.
6. (c) should give both parties an opportunity to mend fences without it necessarily being the prime purpose of the call.
7. (b) is best since you should always adopt a 'business as usual' approach until the other person decides to share a confidence with you.
8. (c) on the basis that discretion is the better part of valour.
9. (b) is usually possible if you choose your words with care, for example by ensuring that you don't directly contradict him but simply offer an alternative point of view.
10. (b) is probably the most practical but maybe you should be looking round for a job in a company more suited to your personality.

CHAPTER 4
Handling Business Meetings

Three or more people discussing business together constitute a meeting. Many such meetings are *informal*, being held to consider a particular problem or opportunity, while others are *formal*, being held on a regular basis with a specific purpose and agenda.

Whether informal or formal all business meetings are more effective if those involved understand and follow some straightforward rules of procedure and etiquette. Many meetings are too long, poorly focused or inconclusive because one or more of the participants fails to observe them.

Judge whether you are helping or hindering the success of the meetings you attend by studying the guidelines given below and then completing the simple self-assessment test.

Informal meetings

These may be *prearranged* ('Let's get together with Mike from Accounts in my office at four o'clock to see if we can sort the problem out') or *impromptu* ('I've asked Bill and Jim to join us to decide how to answer the query from head office').

There are seven golden rules for organising and running a *prearranged meeting*:

1. The *person calling the meeting* (the 'convenor') should be the most senior of those involved or the person with the spending authority (for example, a customer calling a meeting with a supplier). If the participants are of the same seniority, the meeting should be called by the person with the most

direct and urgent interest in the issue to be discussed. A junior should not call meetings involving more senior people – that should be done by his boss.

2. The convenor should decide the *venue and timing* but should always consult the other attendees to make sure it is convenient for them (bearing in mind the urgency of the issue involved).

3. The convenor must say what is the *purpose* of the meeting, *how long* it is expected to last and whether or not any *preparation* is needed ('Please make sure you've seen an analysis of the area sales figures for the last quarter').

4. All those attending should *arrive promptly*. It is not only bad manners to be late but also wastes other people's time and money. Arriving late doesn't prove anything (for example, that you are an important and busy person) except that you are badly organised!

5. The convenor should make the meeting as *short and effective* as possible. If it's been called to issue instructions or to communicate a decision, the convenor does most of the talking. If it's to discuss a problem or opportunity, everyone should be encouraged to participate with the convenor making it clear at the end what he has decided to do. Issues such as follow-up action, which can be discussed on a one-to-one basis, should be deferred until after the meeting.

6. Someone at the meeting should be asked to *record decisions* and major action points. This is often the task of the most junior participant who can get 'Brownie points' by volunteering. Notes should be prepared as quickly as possible (within 48 hours is a good guide), be approved in draft by the convenor if important issues are involved, and circulated to those attending.

7. After the meeting, *communication* with all those likely to be affected by its outcome is essential. This might be done by circulation of the meeting notes, by E-Mail or orally if that is agreed at the meeting. It is vital to include all those who need to know about the outcome since many business problems and inefficiencies stem directly from managers

and staff working in blissful ignorance of a change of policy or priority decided at an informal meeting of which they knew nothing!

Impromptu meetings are often called by a boss with several of his staff or by a senior manager with his colleagues in other disciplines. They almost always interfere with other people's work schedules and are often poorly prepared and inconclusive. If you are about to call an impromptu meeting, the key question to ask before you pick up the phone is: *'Does this have to be dealt with immediately or will it wait until I can set up a proper meeting?'* Lack of consideration in calling impromptu meetings is a major cause of dissatisfaction in many organisations – particularly where tough work targets are set – and many bosses are criticised for putting their own convenience before the efficiency of their staff. So, when in doubt, don't call a meeting.

Impromptu meetings are generally the least formal of any meetings. They may be used to unwind at the end of a busy day or to brainstorm new ideas. If they are focused on a particular issue (for example, reallocating work in the face of a production bottleneck) they are likely to be dealing with topics familiar to the participants and can be simple and action-centred. You should always, however, bear in mind the golden rules for prearranged meetings because your impromptu meeting may turn out to be more important than you originally intended.

Formal meetings

The etiquette of formal meetings (departmental meetings, management meetings, liaison meetings, board meetings and the like) is often perplexing, even to old hands. It is particularly important if you are a 'new boy', to make sure that you understand the rules to avoid appearing naive or inexperienced.

Formal meetings operate on the basis of a *regular timetable* (weekly, monthly, quarterly and so on), are run by an appointed *chairman* (or chair or chairperson in some cases), have precirculated *minutes, agendas and reports* and have a *secretary* who looks after their administration. They usually have an established way of conducting their business which sometimes involves *resolutions* and *voting* (there are, for example, strict rules laid down by law about how companies must conduct shareholders' meetings). If you are new to the group, it is crucial that you understand how each of these issues is organised in the particular case (perhaps by asking the secretary) before your first meeting.

In any event, you should follow these guidelines:

1. *Prepare* for the meeting by reading the last set of minutes, the agenda and any precirculated reports. If you want to raise a topic which is not on the agenda, you can usually do so orally under the heading 'Any other business', but if it involves anything complicated or of major principle, you should ask for the item to be added to the agenda and your submission precirculated at least three working days before the meeting. It is *bad practice* to hand out a board paper at the meeting itself and to expect a decision at that meeting.

2. *Dress formally* (smart business clothes) unless it is clear that this is not expected, and *arrive promptly*. Ideally, aim to be at the venue at least five minutes early – ten minutes if it's your first meeting. Little irritates a chairman more than having to delay the start of a meeting for a late arrival or to give him a reprise of business already done.

3. Respect the established *seating plan*. Most meetings have a seating plan (usually with the chairman at the head of the table) which has become habitual and it is a bad start for the newcomer if he unwittingly takes the place of a longer established member. Simply wait until the members are about to be seated and ask where would be the best place for you to sit.

4. Acknowledge *welcoming remarks* from the chairman (if it's your first meeting) with a simple 'Thank you' and not a five-minute speech!

5. Allow the *chairman to conduct the meeting* by waiting for him to signal that an item is open for discussion (after, for example, the person submitting a report has presented it). If you are a new member, wait for more senior members to express their opinions before offering your own. *Be brief, courteous and relevant* and, wherever possible, put forward positive rather than purely critical views. Make your comments *to the chair* ('I suggest, Mr Chairman, that the way we should view this problem is', etc) unless it is clear that members are usually addressed directly. Avoid being pompous or stilted in the way that you speak – the fact that the meeting is formal doesn't mean that you shouldn't act naturally.

6. Be *respectful* of your peers and their views, however violently you may disagree with them. Polite and persuasive argument is much more effective than sarcasm or personal abuse. Don't forget that the way you conduct yourself in meetings is often an important factor when promotion decisions are made.

7 Make sure that *conclusions are drawn* on every issue. Although this should be the chairman's job, you may sometimes find that items are left unresolved and it is perfectly proper to ask, for example, whether they are to be carried forward to the next meeting or referred to an individual to consider further. If the custom is to propose and vote on resolutions, remember that you may propose amendments – but only with the permission of the chairman.

8. You should always remember that what is discussed in many formal meetings is *confidential*. It can be a serious breach of etiquette to talk too freely about what went on in a meeting and the reputation of being a 'loose tongue', once gained, is very difficult to shake off.

9. *Minutes* are normally agreed in draft by the chairman before circulation but are not formally adopted until the following meeting. If you think a particular minute is incomplete or inaccurate, it is good practice to alert the chairman to your

concern before the meeting at which they are to be considered.

10. If you strongly disagree with what is being done by the group, you may decide to *withdraw* from a particular meeting or to *resign*. If you withdraw from a meeting, you should ask that your withdrawal is recorded in the minutes so that anything decided after you have left does not necessarily carry your support. If you decide to resign, you should write personally to the chairman stating this intention. You don't need to wait for a meeting to be held for this to become effective. Even after you have left a group, you should regard yourself as being bound by the same ethical principles of loyalty and confidentiality as you were when you belonged to it.

Business meals

Working breakfasts, lunches and dinners are an established way of doing business. They have their own code of behaviour which you should observe if you are to get the best out of them.

If you are the *host*, you should use them:

- To establish a new relationship in a very informal way (such as with a potential customer or trading partner or somebody you've only previously dealt with by letter)
- To explore a business proposition in a discreet way without the pressures of the office environment (often used for recruitment interviews)
- To get to know someone better personally (maybe a colleague or business associate)
- To discuss a personnel issue with a subordinate (promotion, job transfer, early retirement, etc)
- To fit in a meeting in either your (or your guest's) over-burdened schedule.

If you are the *guest* you'll probably have a fairly good idea of why you're being asked – remember the old adage that 'there's no such thing as a free lunch'. If you are uncertain, ask politely before you meet so that you can do any homework that's required.

The host usually (but not invariably) *invites* the guest personally by telephone but should *always* confirm the date, time and venue in writing. If the guest is likely to be unfamiliar with the location, he should include clear directions in the letter. If the host is going to be accompanied by colleagues, he should state this in the letter and give their job title or function ('I shall be joined by Ted Slater who is in charge of our Cardiff branch'). It is courteous for the host or his secretary to call the guest a few days before the event to confirm the arrangements.

The host should always be at the venue ten minutes ahead of the meeting to *confirm the dining arrangements* with the restaurant or hotel. The host should greet the guest personally (don't leave this to a hall porter or head waiter) and should ensure that the guest is comfortable before going in to eat.

It is conventional for the host to decide when and how the *business topic* is introduced. It is usual for the early part of the meal to be concerned with general and social issues (not least to get the ordering of the food out of the way), with more serious business matters being raised later. If there is more than one member in the host's party, it is helpful for them to agree a broad agenda and timetable for the business part of the meal. Hosts should always brief themselves on the guest's background (both of his company and personally). They should always ensure that the guest enjoys the meal as much as possible and not let the business discussion distract them from their role as host.

Business meals are almost always informal in structure although brief *notes of actions or decisions* are often made at their conclusion. *Business cards* are usually exchanged at the end of business meals rather than at the beginning. The host should always *pay* for the meal and this should be done as discreetly as possible (ideally by signing an account to be charged to his company and *never* with a flurry of notes and coins). However, it is not usual to pay the guest's taxi fare back to his office or hotel.

Business meals are quite unsuitable for meetings where working papers and files are likely to be needed. It is impossible to manipulate a lever arch file and a knife and fork at the same time and the result is usually neither a satisfactory meeting nor an enjoyable meal.

It is mandatory for the guest to write promptly and personally *thanking the host* for the meal (even if the fish disagreed with him!). Letters with handwritten salutations and valedictions ('Dear John and 'Yours, Tim') are best and should *never* be signed by a secretary. They should be kept short (unless there's a good business reason for writing at more length) and should always include the words 'Thank you' somewhere.

Social occasions

There are numerous occasions when your business life and your social life become intermingled. These events include:

- Meals at home with colleagues or business associates
- Business hospitality events
- Office parties and similar functions
- Weddings and funerals.

Each can represent a minefield of potential *faux pas* for the unwary.

Business entertaining at home usually involves the host and his guests' partners and can range from a homely supper for a visiting colleague from another town to a full dress dinner for the board of a newly acquired subsidiary. Obviously, the approach to one is likely to be very different from the other. None the less, some basic principles apply to all such occasions:

1. The courtesies of invitation are the same as for any business meal (see above). However, the host must also check his

guests' *dietary requirements* – discovering too late that you are presenting roast beef to a strict vegan can be embarrassing to say the least!

2. It is usually bad manners and boring to those not involved to *discuss business* except in general terms or as an excuse for an anecdote which will appeal to everyone. It is particularly embarrassing to be a guest when the host tries to use the intimacy of the domestic surroundings to clinch a deal that should be discussed in the office. The days when the ladies retired after dinner are long past (thank goodness) and the host should remember that a meal at home is meant primarily to be an enjoyable occasion.

3. Hosts and guests and their partners should *act naturally*, however strong the temptation to do otherwise (particularly if the guests are the boss and his wife). This includes offering simple but well-prepared food rather than elaborate failures. The host should judge what will best please his guests and meet that expectation. Equally, the guests should respond amicably to what the host offers. It is as thoughtless for a guest to hog the conversation with accounts of his last holiday as it is for a host to insist on watching his favourite TV programme.

4. It is customary for the guest to bring a *small gift* on arrival (chocolates or something similar) and perhaps to send flowers as an additional thank-you after the event.

Hospitality events

These are increasingly common and may involve you, either as host or guest, in a sporting, cultural or activity event. The idea is to combine business with pleasure and the general principles outlined above should be followed. There are, however, one or two additional points to be watched for if you are the host:

- Try to match your guests to the event (four hours of Wagner at Covent Garden may not be to everyone's taste).
- Always make sure that your guest knows the expected form

of dress (rather different for Henley Regatta and clay pigeon shooting).

- Never ply your guests with alcohol if they are driving to the event (alternatively, many hosts arrange taxis or buses for their guests).
- Make sure that you enjoy the event too (it is disconcerting for a guest if the host is too absorbed in dispensing hospitality).

Office parties and the like

Many people regard office parties as opportunities to unwind, to take a rise out of colleagues and bosses and perhaps indulge in amorous adventures which would not be possible during normal hours. In many organisations they are like tribal rituals which one suspects no one actually enjoys.

Joining in these business events is normally expected of the individual if he is not to be branded as being aloof. Clearly, there are great benefits to be gained if these occasions are well organised – the problems arise when they get out of hand.

The golden rules for surviving office parties are as follows:

- Stay sober.
- Don't gossip or be indiscreet.
- The more senior you are, the earlier you should leave.
- Don't hold post mortems or remind people the next day of what they said or did.

If you find you've seriously transgressed these rules, for example by being rude to a colleague, *make your apologies* as fully and as rapidly as possible. Most people will forgive and forget an indiscretion that is freely acknowledged. Pretending it never happened just makes you look foolish.

Weddings and funerals

The etiquette of being a good guest at a colleague's *wedding* is little different from that of any other wedding except that:

- You should be discreet about the invitation since other colleagues may not have been invited.
- Your working relationship may give you opportunities to be of special help to him in preparing for the event.
- If the bride or groom is your boss, you will need to behave in a way which reassures them that you will not take advantage of your personal friendship in the work context.

Funerals of close colleagues or business associates must take precedence over all other business commitments. It is usual for an organisation to send a wreath or donation to a chosen charity in its own name but *letters of condolence*, whether to the deceased person's company or next of kin, should be handwritten by appropriate individuals including its most senior person (for example, chairman or managing director). It is customary for letters of condolence to include the words 'this letter does not require a reply' although, equally customarily, they are acknowledged by the recipient.

It is no longer usual for non-family members to observe any form of mourning excepting the convention of sobre dress at funerals and memorial services and the flying of a flag at half mast for a day when the death of a very senior person occurs.

If you represent your company at the funeral of a business associate, you should remember to familiarise yourself with the whole relationship with the deceased person – not just your own acquaintance with him. This will enable you to deal sensitively and appropriately with his business colleagues and family.

Assess your own performance

This chapter has covered a wide range of issues relating to business meetings. Complete the following checklist and rate your performance by referring to the scores on page 56.
Always = 5, Sometimes 3, Never = 1.

	Always	**Sometimes**	**Never**

1. I only call informal meetings when the subject is sufficiently important to justify taking people's time.

2. I let people know about the subject to be discussed and how long the meeting is likely to last.

3. I expect meetings to start promptly and ensure that I arrive in good time.

4. I make it a practice to let people know the outcome of the informal meetings that I hold.

5. When I'm in charge of a meeting I make sure that everyone keeps to the point.

6. I don't waste my colleagues' time by casual visits except when I know that they're not busy.

7. I expect to receive papers well in advance of regular, formal meetings.

8. I read all the relevant papers before I arrive at a meeting.

9. I let the chairman know before the meeting if I disagree with the minutes of the previous one.

Business Etiquette

	Always	Sometimes	Never

10. I don't try to dominate meetings and allow others to express their views fully.

11. I respect confidential information that I have learned in meetings and abide by decisions, even if I disagree with them.

12. I behave in a good-humoured and constructive way aimed to maintain the goodwill of my colleagues.

13. I don't lose my temper in meetings, shout at colleagues or resort to sarcasm or innuendo.

14. If I'm organising a business meal, I confirm the arrangements in writing with my guests.

15. I arrive at a business meal engagement at least ten minutes before my guest(s).

16. I write a personal note to thank my host after attending a business meal.

17. I check any dietary requirements of my business guests before entertaining them at home.

	Always	**Sometimes**	**Never**

18. I avoid discussing business when in the company of my own and my guests' partners.

19. I take a small gift when I am being entertained by a business contact at his home.

20. I try to invite guests who will have interests in common and are likely to get on well together.

21. I take my responsibilities as host very seriously and ensure that my guests have all they need.

22. I provide an alternative to alcohol and don't press my guests to drink if I know that they are driving.

23. I keep myself under control at office parties and make sure that I behave correctly.

24. I don't remind my colleagues of their indiscretions after office parties.

25. I keep in touch with the personal lives of my business contacts and write to them when notable events occur.

Checklist scores

Add up your total score (maximum 125) and compare your rating as follows:

100–125   You obviously behave in an exemplary way in business meetings and would make an ideal chairman of the board!

75–100   An excellent score which probably typifies most caring managers. You can do better but you already have a head start.

50–75   There is lot of scope for improvement and you should think very carefully about how your behaviour impacts on your colleagues.

25–50   You have a serious problem with being involved with other people in the context of business. Maybe you should reassess your attitude towards working in a business team.

CHAPTER 5
The Etiquette of the Written Word

The way you write has a huge influence over your success (or failure) in business. Your letters, memoranda, reports or submissions to E-Mail all contribute evidence of your competence in your job. It isn't just a matter of expressing your ideas clearly and persuasively.

A letter which is incorrectly addressed or which adopts an inappropriate tone can easily have the unintentional effect of upsetting the reader. You must ensure that your reader is in a receptive frame of mind. Failure to observe the appropriate etiquette in what you write can create an unseen barrier between you and the reader which, at worst, can result in an undeserved hostility towards you and your communication.

Handling the etiquette of the written word involves following some simple principles, the most important of which is that: **Before you write, think about the reader.**

This sounds obvious but too many writers:

- *Incorrectly address* the recipient
- Write *too lengthy* or *technically complex* letters or memoranda
- Adopt an *inappropriate style* for the subject concerned.

It is clear that they are more concerned in having the subject dealt with from their standpoint than achieving effective communication with the recipient. The result is often both inefficient and irritating.

In this chapter we explore some of the basic elements which represent good etiquette in *business correspondence* and *internal memoranda*.

Business correspondence

Levels of confidentiality

Much business correspondence is addressed by one individual to another without any restriction on its confidentiality. This indicates that the writer is unconcerned with who sees the letter in the recipient's office or effectively who deals with it. Thus, a letter addressed to 'The Chief Buyer, Acme Foods Limited' might be dealt with by a buying clerk if the matter is routine.

If the writer wants to restrict the letter to a named individual, he may mark it (and the envelope) *'Confidential'* or *'Private & confidential'* on the assumption that only the individual (and his secretary) will see the letter and respond to it. It is courteous for the recipient to use the same level of confidentiality when responding.

If the writer wants the recipient to open the letter personally it should be marked *'Personal'* or *'Private'*. This form should only be used for genuinely confidential matters (such as correspondence about employment) and it is often appropriate for the letter itself to be handwritten rather than typed.

The highest levels of confidentiality are letters marked *'Secret'* or *'For your eyes only'* although some argue that these restrictions draw undue attention to the material they contain.

As a general rule you should choose the level of confidentiality appropriate to the subject matter rather than to the person to whom you are writing. Thus, there will be some occasions when an 'open' form is right and others when you wish to limit the readership.

Remember that *fax transmissions* are always in open format (however you mark them) unless you specifically ask the recipient to attend the machine personally.

Modes of address

The first rule is always to *spell the recipient's name and address correctly*. Approximations will not do! Names are very precious to people and time spent in getting them right (consult directories or secretaries to check them) is well invested. This should include making sure that the recipient's titles, honours and qualifications are correctly recorded on both the letter and the envelope.

Much business correspondence is conducted on the basis of the *'Dear Sir/Yours faithfully'* mode with the text written in the third person ('We have received your order of 24th August which will be despatched to you within the next seven days'). This is perfectly correct for routine matters but is somewhat impersonal and inappropriate for dealing with queries and complaints.

More common and flexible is the *'Dear Mr Boothroyd/Yours sincerely'* style in which both the writer and the recipient are named. Such letters should always be written in the first person ('I was glad to receive your kind comments about our recent exhibition') and the ugly construction of referring to the writer in the third person ('In the humble opinion of the writer') never used. It is sometimes difficult, from previous correspondence, to deduce the sex of the writer or, equally problematically, whether a lady should be addressed as Mrs, Miss or Ms. If it proves impossible by research to find out which is correct, the writer should choose the most probable form and start the letter by saying, for example, 'I have addressed you as Mrs Johnson and I am not sure whether this is correct or not. If it is not, please accept my apologies. Perhaps you could let me know when you reply what we should record in our address files'.

As business acquaintances become more familiar, it is common to use a phrase such as *'Kind regards'* before 'Yours sincerely'. This expression of esteem should always be used in subsequent correspondence since its omission might well be taken to indicate a cooling of the relationship.

Personal letters between business friends are often styled *'Dear Peter/Yours John'*, both the salutation and the valediction being handwritten.

It is important to address dignitaries such as peers, ambassadors, academics, bishops and holders of other high offices in the appropriate form. The best sources of reference on this subject are appendices to good dictionaries and the annual *Whitaker's Almanack*.

Formal and informal styles

A formal style of correspondence is right for a large proportion of business transactions. It usually involves individuals who have never met and who are fulfilling routine but important functions for their organisations. The important point of etiquette is to apply a consistent and clear approach which combines courtesy with business efficiency. Using a formal style should not be an excuse for churlishness or bad manners. Thus, a formal letter should say, 'We are grateful for your order which will receive our immediate attention' and not 'We are in receipt of yours of 24th inst which is receiving attention'. While the latter is not rude it is hardly reader-friendly!

After writing a formal letter, read it over and ask yourself, *'Would I say this if I met the recipient in person?'* If the answer is 'No', rewrite the letter.

Informal styles are almost always adopted for non-routine correspondence and are always used between business acquaintances who know each other personally (however acrimonious the subject matter might be!). The writer in this style has to tread a careful path between being too friendly and too coolly businesslike. The most reliable approach is to signal the 'personal' content of the letter by a separate paragraph, either at the beginning or at the end of the letter. Thus, you might say, for example, 'Margery and I thoroughly enjoyed our day on the river with you and Ruth last Sunday. It was very clever of you to arrange such splendid weather!' at the end of a businesslike letter discussing the merits of a new pricing structure.

Writing informally offers the benefit of allowing your own personality and ideas to be directly communicated to the recipient. Whenever possible you should *sign such letters personally* (only allowing them to be signed 'pp' when that is unavoidable) and should *always proof-read them before despatch*. In these days of wordprocessor power it is unconvincing to receive a letter marked 'dictated by Mr Evans but signed in his absence'.

Using humour in business letters
It is often tempting to lighten a business letter with an element of humour, particularly if you know the recipient well. The possibilities range from simple jokes to ironic or sarcastic observations about something or someone of mutual acquaintance.

Although this sounds very innocent, the soundest rule to follow is *when in doubt, leave it out*! The reasons are simple:

- Although the letter may leave you in a cheerful mood it may be received in the middle of a crisis when even the sharpest wit is unwelcome.
- The written word is often open to many different interpretations over which the writer has no control.
- Even though the letter may be addressed to one individual who will share the joke, it is likely to be read by colleagues to whom the humour may seem inappropriate.

Equally, irony and sarcasm should never be used as writing techniques to make a business point. For example, saying, 'We were thrilled to receive your order for six dozen egg boxes and the chairman has ordered a new Jaguar on the strength of it' may seem to you a timely dig in the ribs for an under-performing customer but is likely to be seen by them as being in very poor taste.

Copy letters
In the great majority of cases in which you send a copy of a letter to another person (either in your or the recipient's organisation) you should *indicate this clearly* at the foot of the letter itself ('cc Accounts Department, Western Area Coordinator, etc'). When dealing with routine issues this saves the recipient from the uncertainty of who is up to date with the matter in hand and

also puts the individuals or departments receiving copies on notice that follow-up action may be expected (unless it is marked 'For information only').

Sending copies to more senior people can sometimes be seen as an aggressive act, indicating, for example, that you have no confidence in the authority of the recipient. To avoid an incorrect impression you should always refer to any exceptional copies in the body of the letter (for example, you might say, 'I am sending a copy of this letter to your sales director for information since he specifically asked me to do so when we met last Friday').

If you don't want the recipient to know who has had copies of a letter, you should use the 'blind' method, involving only you keeping a record of the recipients of copies. This approach is often used where some form of dispute is under way. It has its dangers – not least that the recipient will learn second hand of the wider circulation of a letter they thought was personal to them with a consequential erosion of trust between the parties.

Some people use 'blind' copies as a matter of routine. It is both *bad practice and poor etiquette.*

Responding to letters
Letters should always be responded to *promptly.* In normal business terms that means within five working days of receipt – even if it is only a simple acknowledgement to confirm to the writer that his letter has arrived safely. Many companies use standard acknowledgement slips (sent by letter or fax) which, while somewhat impersonal, reassure the writer that action is in hand. Secretaries should always acknowledge letters on behalf of their boss when he is likely to be away for more than a few days.

Replies should be *personal* where this is required, both as regards content and signature. Writers are unimpressed by people who claim to be too important or too busy to attend to their correspondence.

It is courteous to reply to the *issues raised by the writer in the same order*, responding simply and sincerely to each of them.

Much protracted correspondence would be avoided if this simple maxim was more frequently followed.

Replies should *deal honestly* with the writer; thus, if the recipient can't answer a question, he should say so, or if an apology is warranted, it should be offered without reservation.

Handling conflict in letters

Correspondence is a very imperfect medium for resolving conflict, but is often used as the battleground. Lawyers specialise in handling the drafting of letters aimed to resolve *'Without prejudice'* disputes between individuals and companies, and their services should always be called on when major issues are involved. Very many disputes are the subject of everyday business correspondence and there are rules of etiquette to be observed in those cases.

If you *initiate the conflict,* you should:

- *Set out your case simply and clearly* to the appropriate person in the organisation at fault.
- Offer whatever *supporting information* is required and indicate your availability to provide more information or to attend meetings if needed.
- *Indicate a time-scale* by which you expect the matter to be resolved, failing which the action you then intend to take.
- Take the conflict to the *most senior level* in the organisation (chairman or managing director) if the above fails to provide a solution.

If you are *on the receiving end* of the conflict, you should:

- *Inform* relevant *senior colleagues* and enlist their help if needed.
- *Submit all your letters in draft* to a senior person for a second opinion and, if appropriate, get them to initial copies before despatch.
- *Stick to the facts* and the merits of the case and do not allow your emotions to be apparent in what you write (outbursts

of temperament often indicate to the recipient that the writer has lost the argument).

- *Be patient and courteous.* Very many conflicts prove to be no more than storms in a tea cup and the correspondence file should stand as a testament to the coolness and efficiency with which you handled them.

Internal memoranda

When they should be used

Many managers use the internal memorandum as a dumping ground for any odd thoughts, concerns or random information which may (or as likely may not!) be of interest to their colleagues. These random memorandum producers are a menace. They are also abusing a cardinal rule of good business etiquette: *Be considerate of your colleagues' time.* This rule provides the acid test of when memoranda should be used.

A memorandum is justified if:

- You need a *record of a decision,* a conversation or a piece of information which will be of reference value.
- You're *putting forward a proposition* or plan which needs careful consideration (for example, before a meeting) or which needs the involvement of several people in different locations.
- The topic is one to be considered *out of office hours.*

Modern technology has (unfortunately) facilitated the production of memoranda and their widespread distribution to the extent that they now seriously inhibit the efficiency of many companies in which managers spend a disproportionate amount of time on this form of corporate 'navel gazing'.

The potential writer of a memorandum should ask himself:

- Could I deal with this equally well by *telephone?*
- Would a *handwritten note* be better?
- Am I adding *essential (or inessential) information* to the business?

Memorandum content

If preparing a memorandum is unavoidable, the writer's main obligation is to ensure that the impact of it on the reader is as effective as possible. To achieve this he should:

- Head the memorandum with its degree of *urgency and confidentiality* (for example, 'Background reading on the US market' or 'Essential reading before our meeting next Tuesday – strictly confidential'). This enables the reader to sort out his own priorities without having to scan the text.
- Start the memorandum with a *one-paragraph summary* of what it contains or its main conclusion (for example, 'In this paper I am proposing that we should close the depot in Axminster and transfer our western operations to Taunton'). The fact that writers sometimes find it difficult to summarise their ideas underlines the importance of this recommendation.
- Write *briefly and logically* with plenty of paragraph headings and other aids to the reader (for example, explanations of technical words used).
- *Read over and edit* the memorandum before it is sent, eliminating anything which is not essential (remember that the readers' time is valuable – whatever their role in your business).

Memorandum avoidance

It is tempting to prepare a memorandum at the end of every discussion or telephone call and, indeed, some organisations thrive on this culture of corporate record-keeping. The justification claimed for this is the importance of having hard copy data should disputes occur. This is true, up to a point, but in most cases a brief summary, if one is needed, is just as well recorded by hand at the time than produced (at length) several days later. In some cases it makes good sense not to have records of unimportant or transient issues, costing money to draft and process and then cluttering up endless filing cabinets.

Robert Townsend, on taking over as president of Avis in the 1970s, waged a successful campaign against the internal memorandum in the company. Good managers follow in this tradition of 'memorandum avoidance', using more immediate and direct means of communication with their colleagues. Once again good etiquette (being considerate of your colleagues' time) coincides with good business practice.

Memorandum circulation
Choose your circulation list according to the following criteria:

- Include those who *need to take action* or have to *be consulted*.
- Include those who *need to be informed* because they have an interest in the outcome of a decision.
- Include those whose *seniority* makes it courteous (or diplomatic) to keep in the picture (usually 'for information').
- *Exclude everyone else.*

Photocopiers have made it remarkably easy to spray copies of memoranda around organisations on the basis that 'if everyone has a copy no one can complain of lack of communication'. The originator of this scatter-gun approach usually learns (to his cost) that his really important memoranda go unread, being buried in a welter of the irrelevant. A simple and courteous device for dealing with potential recipients who are on the margin of the cirulation list is to alert them to the existence of the memorandum and to offer them a copy *should they want one*.

Memoranda as organisational weapons
It is bad etiquette to use a memorandum as a means of criticising or scoring points off a colleague. The technique commonly used is to copy a critical memorandum to the recipient's boss (or other senior colleague) in the expectation that it will cause trouble for him. Personal criticism or disputes between colleagues should be conducted in person, face to face, and not in writing. A memorandum allows no immediate response from the reader and his reaction is invariably to respond with a written salvo in like form. The result is trench warfare by memorandum.

Some unscrupulous managers use the susceptibility of their colleagues to being upset in this way to their own advantage. Managers should be on their guard to spot this abuse of the internal channels of communication within their business.

E-Mail

All the advice given in this chapter on the use and abuse of memoranda applies equally to E-Mail and other forms of electronic post-box systems. The technology often tempts people to overuse the quick and simple facilities which it offers. The fact that you can get a message into a thousand people's mailboxes at the press of a button doesn't make it any less burdensome for those who have to read something of marginal or no interest to them. Once again, the best approach to efficient (and courteous) communication is to alert your potential audience to the availability of your memorandum and leave it to them to decide whether or not to read it.

Putting theory into practice – an exercise

Let's imagine that you have to write a particularly tricky letter. You are the manager of a DIY store, a branch of a national chain, and you lead a hectic, but enjoyable, business life. You have won early promotion and are rightly proud of your success. One morning you receive a call from the company secretary at head office warning you that you'll receive a faxed copy of a letter addressed to the chairman, received that morning, to which you'll be expected to make a prompt reply. The letter is from the managing director of a very large company (a household name) and reads as follows:

Dear Sir John,

I am writing to record a serious complaint about the behaviour of a member of your staff at your Anytown branch. My wife visited that store last week to buy some decorative plaster moulding for our library. Needing assistance, she sought help from several of your staff without success and finally asked to see the manager.

The young person she was speaking to told her in colourful language that the manager was not to be troubled with such trivial matters and, in any case, was not in the habit (to quote his words) of 'dealing with batty old women'. You can imagine her distress and my anger when learning of this event.

I am sure, Sir John, that you will share my belief that this type of behaviour is quite unacceptable and that you will take any necessary disciplinary action.

Yours, etc

Benjamin Hardcastle

The chairman had written back by return of post expressing regrets and promising action. His instruction to you (after some colourful words of reproof) is to ascertain the facts and write to Mr Hardcastle with an appropriate apology. You investigate the incident and find that the culprit is a junior trainee who had been in the branch less than a week. You give him a dressing down and remind all staff of the need for courtesy when dealing with customers. You are convinced that it is an isolated incident but now have to write that letter to Mr Hardcastle. What should you say?

Why not try drafting a reply before looking at the suggested letter which appears opposite.

Dear Mr Hardcastle,

I learned with alarm and concern of the quite unacceptable treatment of your wife when she visited this store last week. I offer you an unreserved apology, both on my own behalf as branch manager and on behalf of the company which always strives to meet the highest standards of customer care.

I have investigated the circumstances in which your wife was so discourteously dealt with and find that the employee concerned is a junior trainee with very short service with us. I appreciate that this does not excuse either his bad manners or our inability to give your wife the guidance she needed when she spoke to other members of my staff. The employee has been reprimanded and all staff reminded of the standards of behaviour that we expect of them.

I am very sorry that this incident occurred and hope that you and your wife will not regard it as anything other than an isolated incident that we much regret.

Yours sincerely

CHAPTER 6
The Etiquette of the Telephone

Hundreds of millions of telephone calls are made every day. A high percentage are made in connection with business and of that huge number a large proportion are between individuals who have never met each other. Calls are made to gain or give information, to discuss and resolve problems, to seek and give advice, to make arrangements and to persuade the listener to take some action. Telephone calls leave no 'footprint' except the recollection in the minds of the parties involved of whether they were effective in meeting their objective.

Many calls are unsatisfactory, leaving one or other party feeling uneasy or irritated (or worse). Quite often the reason for this was not the content of the call but the way it was conducted – in a word, one party failed to observe the normal etiquette that most of us have come to regard as acceptable. Someone handles us badly – our hackles rise – we stop listening – we hang up in a bad temper. The sequence is only too familiar. In this chapter we explore the etiquette of the telephone, discovering that it is as often our unconscious actions which are bad manners as our more obvious errors.

Initiating a call

Like all effective business actions a telephone call needs preparation – well before you lift the handset. Imagine that you have decided to call Mr Jones, the factory manager of your main supplier, to raise a query about a consignment of material. What preparation should you do?

Ask yourself the following key questions:

- Am I clear about *the exact query* that I'm raising and can I put it simply and clearly?
- Have I to hand *all the information* I might need to have a satisfactory discussion with Mr Jones?
- Is Mr Jones *the most appropriate person* to deal with this issue? If not, whom should I approach?
- Is this likely to be *a convenient time* to call Mr Jones (many managers have well-known busy periods in their schedules)?
- *Do I really need to deal with this now* by telephone or would some other method (for example, an exchange of faxes) be more effective?

These questions apply when the call is important or urgent from the point of view of the caller. Equally, there are circumstances in which the call is more important to the receiver (for example, when a bidder is waiting to hear the outcome of a tender) than to the caller. In these cases the responsibility of the caller is to think first about the receiver's interest rather than his own. This is a good example of the 'duty of courtesy' which businessmen owe to each other.

Good preparation is all about making the call as effective as possible, in particular by respecting the time of the receiver. By making the call you have the initiative in shaping the conversation itself. The receiver will always listen for a short time without interrupting the caller and that opportunity should be used to establish your identity and the purpose of the call clearly. It is discourteous (and generally ineffective) to waffle on for a minute or two before coming to the point. If you are speaking to someone for the first time, lack of clarity and brevity on your part may result in your being given the 'double-glazing salesmen's' treatment – a brisk 'Not today, thank you'.

Switchboards and secretaries

Your call will almost certainly be made via the receiver's switchboard. If you're kept waiting (more than five rings), you should be greeted by an apology. If you are not, you know that the switchboard operators lack training. If your call is not answered after ten rings, it is advisable to hang up and call later (not least because you will be less agitated by the delay).

Greet the operator with 'Good morning', announce your name, 'This is Alan Jarvis of Universal Grindings' and say whom you would like to speak to, 'Could I speak to Mr Crisp of Accounts, please?' These courtesies are as essential when dealing with switchboard operators as they are when speaking to secretaries. Your demeanour in handling anyone in another business reflects not only on your own manners but also on the company you represent.

Switchboards often put a caller *on hold* while the connection is sought (sometimes the nerves of the caller are soothed (?) by synthetic music) and, once again, it is good practice for the operator to say to the caller, 'Sorry to keep you waiting' every 20 seconds or so.

On reaching the secretary, the caller should again announce his name and add a brief word about the purpose of the call. This will help the secretary to decide whether to interrupt her boss if he is in a meeting or on another call. It is sensible for callers to get to know the secretaries of business people whom they regularly contact and to use each telephone call to exchange pleasantries before being put through to their boss. Establishing a friendly relationship often makes the job of both secretary and caller more effective and enjoyable. However urgent the issue, the caller should always take a few moments to speak to the secretary in this way before his call is put through.

Some people get their *secretaries to initiate their calls* and in those cases the routine described above should be followed by the secretary, acting on behalf of her boss. It is always bad manners for the receiver to be on the line before the caller, thus, the caller's secretary should always get him on the line *before* the receiver is put through. If you find yourself on the receiving end of the ill-mannered practice of the receiver waiting on the convenience of the caller – hang up!

Organising a call

If the caller is not known to the receiver, it is essential that his credentials and the purpose of the call are established at the outset. For example, 'Good morning, Mr Crisp. I'm Alan Jarvis of Universal Grindings. I recently took over as chief buyer and I'm calling to check on the details of a credit note etc . . .'.

Telephone calls are intended to be dialogues and the caller should always provide the receiver with opportunities to comment or react to a statement (open questions such as 'Has your company dealt with any similar situations in the past?' are particularly useful).

It is usually the job of the receiver to wrap up the telephone conversation (after all, he's the person who has been interrupted) although the caller may nudge the receiver in that direction. The caller should be diplomatic about how this is done and it is important that the call finishes on a friendly and positive note.

Interrupted calls

If a call is cut off, for whatever reason, it is courteous for the original caller to redial. If the receiver suspends the call (for example to deal with an incoming international call or to respond to a summons by his managing director) it is his responsibility to redial. If, in the latter circumstance, the call back is not made within, say, 15 minutes, his secretary should ring the original caller with an explanation and apology. Callers should not be put on hold by a receiver for anything more than a few seconds without explanation.

Good telephone manners

Callers should not be too familiar or casual with receivers they have never met. Most people are comfortable with callers using their surnames on first contact ('Good morning, Mr Stevens') and do not expect the deference of 'Sir' or 'Madam'. They are usually offended by the uninvited use of first names and jokey or unbusinesslike language. Saying 'Hi, John – how ya doin'? I'm the new big banana in the packing department!' is not the ideal way to establish a good working relationship.

Personal matters have a place in many business telephone conversations, not least to help to reinforce the friendships which are an essential feature of good teamwork. You should always be conscious of the possible time pressures that the receiver is under (and is probably too polite to mention) and keep your comments brief and to the point. It is generally considered inappropriate for those in the junior ranks of an organisation to take the initiative in discussing personal matters with those who are more senior.

Always remember to use 'Please' and 'Thank you' at appropriate points in your business calls. No one should be too busy or senior for these common courtesies to be abandoned.

Receiving calls

Busy people often receive calls at very inconvenient times. They might be preparing for a meeting, catching up on important paperwork or attending to a call of nature! The first line of defence for the receiver is his secretary and there is a well-established code of 'white lies' to explain his non-availability. These usually follow a pause while the secretary checks the position with her boss, out of the caller's hearing (not the hand over the mouthpiece and the shouted, 'John – are you in?').

They include:

- 'Mr Jones is busy at the moment – may I ask him to call you back as soon as he's free?'

- 'Mr Jones is in conference – may I, etc.'
- 'Mr Jones has a colleague with him at the moment – may I, etc.'

Most callers recognise these messages and find them perfectly usual. Less acceptable to both caller and receiver are such responses as:

- 'Mr Jones hasn't turned up yet and I've no idea when he'll be back.'
- 'Mr Jones is too busy to talk to you.'
- 'Mr Jones is in the loo – again!'

Interruptions

Two common interruptions for a receiver are *an internal call* on another line and the *unexpected appearance of a colleague* at his office door (often whispering in a totally distracting way).

The correct response to the first is to ask the caller to excuse you while you deal with the call, explain to the internal caller that you are on an outside line and will call back shortly, and then resume the external call with renewed apologies. Colleagues should be ignored unless the matter is urgent in which case a similar routine to interruption from an internal call should be used.

Secretaries should only interrupt their boss when there is an urgent reason and, even then, by giving him a written note rather than by telephone. Most people would understand if the receiver said, 'Excuse me for a moment, John – Ann has just brought in an important message for me'.

If you do interrupt a call, you should explain the reason to the caller. For example, 'I'm sorry, John, I gather there's a call coming in for me from Tokyo. Would you mind if I took it and called you back?' Don't just say, 'Look, John, something's come up – I'll call you back' and put the telephone down.

Recording calls

If you need to record a telephone call (for example, to check over complicated information at leisure) you should only do so *with the permission of the caller*. Failure to do so, however trivial the subject matter of the call, is a serious breach of the caller's privacy. Some organisations routinely record calls for security reasons. This does not absolve the receiver from telling callers that this is the case the first time a call is made.

Should you suspect that your call is being recorded it is better to ask the other person directly (despite the embarrassment this might cause) than to harbour an unconfirmed suspicion. Of course, the receiver might be recording your call despite denying it – an important reason for always taking care in telephone conversations not to say things that you wouldn't want overheard or written down. Face-to-face conversations are the most secure, followed by letters written to private, and not business, addresses.

Conference calls

The facility to involve several people in a simultaneous telephone conference is extremely useful and the courtesies of such electronic meetings should be the same as those used when people meet in the flesh. In particular, the host of such calls should make sure that all those linked up know exactly the identities and roles of the other participants before serious business is discussed.

This rule of good manners applies particularly to the use of the conference telephone when several people can listen in and contribute to the conversation at the same time. It is very bad manners for the user of the conference facility to fail to tell the other party exactly who is with him, listening in to the call. There are few situations more chilling than learning at the end of what you thought was a fairly private conversation that, unknown to you, someone else had been overhearing it all along.

The correct procedure for the user of the conference facility is as follows:

- At the begining of the call *use the handset* (not the 'squawk box').
- Say to the caller something like, 'I've got George Watson from sales and Desmond Ellis from distribution with me. I'd like to bring them into our discussion on the conference phone if that's OK with you . . .'
- When the caller confirms that he has no objection to this, each participant should say 'Hello' or 'Good morning' to *confirm his presence.*
- Use the handset to close the call.

Security

You should always be concerned about the security of your telephone calls, not only from what might be overheard at your end, but, equally importantly, at the receiver's. Since you can't *see* the person you're calling, you don't know whether they have someone with them or are in an open-plan area or for some reason cannot talk freely. If you have confidential or personal matters to discuss, you should always ask something such as 'Are you free to talk, John?' or 'Is this a good time to talk about our Russian contract?' before you start.

Calls can be overheard at various points in their transmission but the most common is within the caller or receiver's own organisation. Common sense dictates that you should only discuss the most confidential matters face to face and not over the telephone. If you have to do so, you should always use code words and other mutually agreed cryptic expressions.

If you accidentally overhear a confidential telephone conversation, you should always tell the caller. That way they can review their security arrangements to avoid a repetition.

Despite their great usefulness *mobile and cellular phones* are essentially insecure and should not be used for any conversations which carry very confidential information. It is perfectly good manners to remind a caller who forgets this that a more appropriate means of communication should be used.

Assess your own performance

Complete the following questionnaire, by circling your answer, and compare your skills in handling telephone etiquette with the answers on pages 80–81.

1. Returning to your desk you find that there have been a number of telephone messages for you. You only have time to return one or two calls. Would you be most likely to choose: (a) the call made to you by the most senior person; (b) the caller who has been most persistent; (c) the caller who describes his message as urgent; or (d) the call which you suspect could be the most important but which could be the most difficult?

2. You have been avoiding speaking to a particularly troublesome business contact and your secretary has instructions to keep him at bay with appropriate white lies about your availability. Having been told by your secretary that you are abroad on business he unexpectedly calls you on your private line. Do you: (a) blame your secretary for not knowing where you are; (b) tell another white lie about making an unscheduled return; or (c) offer no explanation or excuse?

3. As a switchboard operator you find that an incoming caller has been kept waiting for a long period by an inconsiderate staff member who cannot now be traced. You know the matter is important and have to decide whether to: (a) advise the caller that you will ask your colleague to return the call urgently as soon as he can be found; (b) find another colleague who can take over the call and keep the caller happy while the search is on; or (c) advise the caller to ring back later. What would you do?

4. You learn at the end of a confidential telephone conversation with a customer that the receiver has made a tape recording

of it without your permission. The receiver tells you that he 'likes to have a record of what is said to avoid misunderstandings'. You have to decide whether to: (a) avoid saying anything in future calls which might be contentious; (b) start recording calls yourself as a means of cross-checking if needed; and (c) carry on as before. What would you do?

5. You are interviewing a member of staff when you are interrupted by a call from your boss making a serious complaint about that person's performance. Do you: (a) say 'I've got Alan Piper with me at the moment, Mr Smithers, I'll call you back later, if I may'; (b) say 'Look, it's difficult for me to talk right now, Mr Smithers. I'll call you back'; or (c) listen to what your boss has to say without comment?

6. A personal call from an old friend living abroad is put through to you in the middle of an important business meeting. Do you: (a) ask for the call to be diverted and take it in another room; (b) speak briefly to the caller, explaining that you're in a meeting and will call him back later; (c) ask your secretary to take a message; or (d) take the call but speak quietly and unobtrusively?

7. You are in the middle of a business call when your boss sits down by your desk. You know that the call will take some time yet and that your boss will become irritated if he is kept waiting. Should you: (a) break off the call with a promise to ring later; (b) cover the handset with your hand and whisper to your boss that you'll be some time; or (c) ask your contact to hold on for a moment while you have a brief word with your boss?

8. You receive a very confidential fax which has come to you by mistake, being intended for a competitor. You have to decide whether or not to let the sender and the intended recipient know that it has been misdirected. Would you: (a) tell the sender but not the recipient; (b) tell both; or (c) tell neither?

9. Your firm has a standing instruction that confidential matters shouldn't be discussed on mobile phones. In a momentary

lapse you forget this rule and give some very commercially sensitive data to a customer on your mobile. Should you: (a) say nothing and hope that you were not overheard; (b) report the matter to your company in case there are some repercussions; or (c) in addition to (b) tell the customer as well?

10. You have an experienced switchboard operator who prides herself on the courtesy with which she deals with callers and her unflappability. She has one *bête noire* in the form of a regular caller who is always rude and inconsiderate. She has to decide whether to deal with him: (a) exactly as she does with all other callers and ignore his rudeness; (b) treat him coldly but efficiently and hope that he gets the message; or (c) confront him with the unpleasantness of his manner and risk causing him offence. Which should she do?

Suggested answers to assessment test

1. (c) or (d) are the important priorities: (c) because you know that the caller believes the problem is urgent and (d) because you probably do.

2. (b) is the most diplomatic (as long as it sounds plausible) or (c) if you and the caller are not on the best of terms.

3. (b) shows most initiative and will be applauded by the caller even if your search proves fruitless.

4. (a) is the sensible solution and, if your customer complains that you are not forthcoming on the telephone, you can politely explain why.

5. (a) is best since Alan Piper won't know what is being said and the caller will immediately realise why it is inconvenient for you to talk.

6. (b) is the most courteous from the point of view of those with you in the meeting but revert to (a) if it isn't going to be convenient for the caller to return the call.

7. (c) is the correct approach – most callers will be familiar

with this type of interruption and will excuse you while you deal with it.

8. (a) is the appropriate answer – you should leave it to the sender to explain the circumstances to the intended recipient.

9. (b) is the most practical – there is no reason why you should also alert the other party unless he stands to lose by the call being overheard.

10. (a) is the correct answer since callers seldom welcome their shortcomings being pointed out by people they regard as being junior to themselves.

CHAPTER 7

Being Courteous to Foreign Business People

Different cultures, different customs

Let's assume that you are fully familiar with the rules of good business behaviour in the United Kingdom. Your boss asks you to deal with an important customer from Japan, including entertaining him and his wife. You behave exactly as you would with a local customer but the visit is a disaster. What went wrong?

You made the crucial error of believing that you only need to change your behaviour when visiting people in their own country – in other words, that the overseas visitor should be prepared to adopt our ways when he is here. There are, of course, many aspects of business (working hours, legal and procedural differences, trade practices, and so on) to which the visitor must adapt if he is to succeed. Equally, there are habits and attitudes so deeply engrained in his own culture that he cannot change his reaction if he finds something embarrassing or unacceptable. These can range from behaviour which offends deeply-held religious beliefs to apparently innocuous social habits.

It is the job of the host to make his business guest feel at ease and there is no excuse for not being familiar with the more important aspects of good manners that your visitor will expect from you. You should also find that your guest is impressed by the attention you have given to his needs – and maybe you'll land that Japanese order after all!

Speaking their language

We have the advantage of speaking English as our native tongue, a world language that is widely used in business. We also have an increasing number of people in business who are fluent in at least one other foreign language. For many, however, the likelihood is that he will not be able to speak the language of the visitor he is about to entertain. What should he do?

Here are some simple guidelines:

- *Never assume* that your visitor will be able to converse effectively in English (however slowly and loudly you may speak!) but find out before he arrives if you are likely to have a communication problem.
- If you are likely to need an *interpreter*, look for one first among the staff of your own firm (even if they have no technical input to make to the discussion they will at least understand its general context) before using outside agencies.
- *Confirm with the visitor* that he has no objection to an interpreter being used and check that he is happy with the person chosen; in some very high-level negotiations two sets of interpreters are used but this should be avoided in normal business dealings where the trustworthiness of the other party is not in question.
- Prepare relevant *documents in both languages* and translate minutes and other records into the visitor's language: although this may seem unnecessarily time-consuming it often avoids serious misunderstandings arising through a lack of appreciation of the nuances of English.
- Learn some simple *phrases of greetings and thanks* in your visitor's language. The time and effort involved will be more than repaid by their appreciation of the gesture you make; and why not use a simple speech of welcome written for you in their language?
- *Apologise to your visitor* for not speaking his language, however obscure it might be; don't use interpreters for social occasions since you will almost certainly find that the struggle

to make yourself understood without the benefit of a common language is an excellent way to make friends with your guest.

Key differences in business manners when dealing with . . .

Americans

In meetings

- American men invariably shake hands during introductions – women not so often.
- Punctuality is very important and late attendance at a meeting is regarded as being very discourteous.
- Business cards are not automatically exchanged at meetings – only if there is some reason to get in touch later; no one will refuse your card but don't feel insulted if you are not given one in return.
- Breakfast meetings are popular with Americans (often used for the intimate business get-together) and meetings over lunch (12.30–2.00) are the rule rather than the exception.

Personal style

- On meeting, Americans will often repeat your name out loud as a means of implanting it in their memory (they tend to be much better at this than we are) and immediately use your first name whether or not you have invited them to do so; this is normal business practice and should not be taken as being over-familiar.
- The most common opening line when meeting people socially is 'What do you do?' (viewed as being rather crass in the UK) and you may well be asked what you earn; be prepared for both questions and don't be offended by them.
- Americans have been slightly jumpy about accepting business

gifts since the payola scandals of the 1970s (after all, the head of the National Security Council lost his job for accepting two Japanese watches!) and there is a Federal law which places a limit of $25 on their tax deductibility; when in doubt, avoid gifts but entertain them instead (this causes them no problems with the IRS).

- Americans generally place considerable value on business being conducted in a courteous way, but don't be fooled; they don't regard a deal as done until it's legally enforceable and then are more willing than most to sue anyone who breaches their obligations (in the words of Sam Goldwyn, 'An oral contract ain't worth the paper it's written on!').

Japanese

In meetings

- In Japan the usual greeting is a long, low bow and not a handshake. The bow has a great deal of ritual and taboo attached and is made from the waist, with back and neck stiff, hands sliding down towards the knees and eyes averted; when they visit the UK they will expect only to shake hands and you should not attempt the bow until you and your visitor are reasonably well acquainted.
- Business cards must be exchanged on first meeting and should be offered and accepted with both hands.
- Never address the business visitor by his first name, only family and very close friends do that; use 'Mr . . .' or the Japanese form '. . . san' until invited to be more familiar.
- The Japanese have an aversion to close physical contact, so remember to avoid backslapping or holding an elbow when making a point.
- It is impolite to yawn in public, pointing is done with the entire hand and laughter does not necessarily signify joy or amusement; it can also be a sign of embarrassment.
- Japanese business people are intensely concerned to

observe the hierarchy of their organisations and juniors will always be obedient to their seniors in meetings, waiting to be invited to speak and never openly disagreeing with their boss; it is often regarded as courteous to address the senior person via his junior colleague (particularly if translation is involved) and for the junior to act as the spokesman for his reply.

- It is regarded as impolite for Japanese to say 'No' and you should avoid pressing a question to the point that your visitor has little option but to do so; experience will give you the ability to use phrases which give him an honourable way of turning you down without loss of face.

Personal style

- Wives play little part in Japanese business life and your visitor will normally expect to be entertained on his own; if you are entertaining him at home, you should remember not to ask too many questions about his home life and to avoid topics which might prove embarrassing to him in other ways.
- Japanese place the most importance on gift-giving of all business nations and many regard it as a necessity and not just an optional nicety; never surprise your Japanese guests with a gift since his inability to reciprocate immediately may embarrass him; if you are intending to give a gift to an individual, quietly alert him ahead of time of your intention to give him a memento and present it to him in private (*never* give a gift in a group and ignore the others present); gifts are usually opened in private to avoid excessive emotional display.
- Gifts should be wrapped in pastel-coloured paper (never in white and never with bows); gifts in twos are supposed to bring good luck (cufflinks, pen and pencil sets, and so on) but never in fours (four is also the word for death); try to match the value of the gift to the seniority of the recipient.
- Never send red Christmas cards – funeral notices are posted in red in Japan.

Arabs

In meetings

- The standard greeting in most Arab countries is 'Salaam alayakum' ('peace be upon you') either accompanied, or followed, by a handshake; the right hand may be placed over the heart and your visitor may place his hand on your right shoulder and kiss you on both cheeks (don't offer to do this uninvited).
- Late attendance at meetings is not regarded as discourteous in many Arab countries, particularly when the visitor is richer or more important than the host; it is discourteous to draw attention to your guest's late arrival or to indicate in any way that you are under time pressure.
- It is usual to precede the discussion of business with 'pleasantries' which should avoid contention (such as politics or religion) or intrusion into your guest's private life (don't enquire about his health or family).
- Don't sit in a way which shows your guest the soles of your shoes (regarded as very insulting) or be surprised if your guest removes his shoes in your office (you don't have to follow suit unless you feel like it).
- Be prepared for discussions to take much longer than with western visitors and don't show impatience, however much you may feel it; remember that under Islamic law there are strict rules regarding some aspects of commercial transactions and be prepared to accommodate these before the meeting starts.

Personal style

- Many Arab societies are male dominated and you should not expect to meet and shake hands with a visitor's wife or offer her a gift when visiting them at their hotel.
- The visitor will expect to receive comparable hospitality to

what he would offer you in his own country (which can often be very lavish) and it is important that you don't neglect this; dining out is the most popular form of entertainment, perhaps followed by a night club or a casino if your guest enjoys gambling.

- It is good manners to offer refreshments to your Arab guest as soon as he arrives (tea, coffee, sweet cakes and chocolates are very acceptable) but remember that they usually observe strict dietary rules and would be offended by being offered alcohol.

- In traditional Arab meals the right hand only is used to eat; it is impolite to gesture with the left hand and to point with the finger.

- Holding hands between men is a common show of friendship among Arabs and you should not reject a hand offered to you in this spirit – however strange the experience may seem.

- Unlike in Japan, gift-giving is not of primary importance but rather should be seen as part of the wider significance placed on hospitality; small gifts are common when attending a dinner (typically flowers or sweets) and more expensive gifts to recognise a particular favour (silver, crystal, porcelain and brand-name goods are popular, but avoid handkerchiefs which are associated with tears and parting).

Scandinavians

In meetings

- Conservative dress, formal manners and punctuality are all expected when dealing with Scandinavians; at the outset they may seem stand-offish or unfriendly but this is a natural reserve which is usually overcome with longer acquaintance.

- Some topics – salary, social status and politics – are usually avoided in formal meetings; humour is acceptable but the subject should be carefully chosen to avoid giving offence.

- Remember that relations between different Scandinavian countries are not always cordial and therefore take care not to cause offence by an unthinking generalisation.

Personal style

- Making speeches and toasting your colleagues and guests at dinners are popular activities involving some well-established rituals; toasts are initiated by the host and responded to with 'Skol' and a nod of the head by his fellow diners; after that everyone joins in with a toast of their own!
- Eye contact is important to most Scandinavians and elaborate hand gestures are uncommon: they tend to show much courtesy to women, and men are expected always to walk on a woman's left side.
- Shows of emotion are generally frowned on, personal behaviour tending to be unflamboyant and understated.
- Exchanging business gifts of modest value is acceptable but more extravagant offerings can cause offence.

Continental Europeans

We have much in common with our continental European neighbours and so the differences in culture and business habits are not so marked as with those from further afield. The opening up of Eastern European countries and the component states of the former USSR have introduced new opportunities to do business across European frontiers. What follows is a brief digest of some of the points to watch for.

- **French** businessmen are often more reluctant than many other continental Europeans to use English as the language in which business should be conducted. Shaking hands on parting as well as on meeting is the general habit, however well the individuals know each other. Warmer embraces including the double kiss to the cheeks are common between business acquaintances of the opposite sex. However, slapping on the back or on any other part of the anatomy is regarded as bad-mannered. Humour is rarely a feature of business occasions.

- **Germans** expect a great degree of formality in business dealings. First names are only used when invited and women in business are always addressed as 'Frau' irrespective of their marital status. Senior businessmen are sometimes referred to as 'Herr Doktor' even if they have no formal qualification of that rank. Meetings are usually arranged well in advance and punctuality is at a premium. Humour should be handled with care in meetings with German businessmen and avoided entirely on very formal occasions. Business entertaining is not usually undertaken during the negotiation of a deal since it might be seen to influence the outcome but is quite acceptable afterwards.

- **Dutch** businessmen are generally used to doing business in a number of languages and are usually fluent English speakers. Their approach to business tends to be more relaxed than that of their German neighbours and in most respects is broadly comparable with the UK.

- Both **Italian** and **Spanish** businessmen are likely to be less concerned about the formality and punctuality of meetings than their northern European counterparts. Family life is regarded as being of considerable importance and it is polite to enquire about the family's well-being before business is commenced. Contentious issues can quickly become the subject of heated exchanges although the effect is temporary (this is considered to be quite normal business behaviour). There are no taboos connected with business entertaining and the exchange of appropriate gifts is quite acceptable.

- Businessmen from **eastern European** countries and **Russia** are still familiarising themselves with the normal manners of western business. They have been used to very formal and bureaucratic structures with little expectation that individuals will speak out against the approved line. They may therefore be uneasy about handling themselves appropriately when abroad and find difficulty with some of our accepted customs. It is the job of the host to make their visits successful and it seems likely that significant quantities of alcohol and late nights will be involved. Remember that smoking is still an acceptable and common practice in these countries and, if necessary, you should show special consideration for your visitor's habits.

Ethnic and religious differences

You should respect ethnic and religious differences in your business dealings whether or not the person you are meeting with is a visitor from overseas. If you are asked to meet someone from a country that is unfamiliar to you (whether it's Taiwan, Malawi, Paraguay or anywhere else in the world) you should always research, before they arrive, the background to their country and culture so that you can make their visit as enjoyable and effective as possible. The most striking differences often apply to dress, business customs and diet, and you should be prepared to respond appropriately to their needs. You should never show that you are surprised or embarrassed by their expectations and should make sure that your colleagues are properly briefed. Most visitors will expect to adapt their style to our ways, but showing knowledge and consideration for what will make them feel at home will do a great deal for your credibility and the success of your relationship.

Religious requirements should not be ignored. For example, Orthodox Jews will not wish to transact any business on the Sabbath or during religious holidays and Muslims will not wish to eat or drink (or see you doing so) during Ramadan. Both Jews and Muslims have strict dietary laws and you should avoid giving offence by offering them unsuitable food or drink. Many business people no longer regard alcohol as being an appropriate accompaniment to meals and it is often safer (and healthier!) to offer only soft drinks.

You should always avoid jokes or humorous anecdotes

involving religious topics even though these might be volunteered by your guest about his own religion. It is surprisingly easy to give offence with an ill-chosen story.

You should always take your duties as host very seriously and it is better to be excessively courteous rather than appear abrupt or patronising. You should not forget that many visitors still hold memories of 'Imperial Britain' and may take as a slight any thoughtless remark or action on your part. Be modest about yourself, your company and country, and all should be well.

Summing up

Dealing with visitors from other countries should be one of the most interesting and rewarding things you have to do. If you organise your duties as host well and are ready to deal with the unexpected without getting into a flap, you should do good business too!

CHAPTER 8
Business to Business

The courtesies which are commonplace in the dealings between individuals should apply equally to the relationships between businesses. The assumption that a business has no personality is false. The reality is that, when dealing with other companies, *every action of every employee creates an image* which either reinforces the expected standards of behaviour of the business or detracts from it. It makes good business sense for everyone to behave in a consistent way because:

- Suppliers, customers and competitiors respect companies that *place consideration for others high on their agenda*
- It encourages *more effective team performance* and
- Is good for *morale.*

When dealing 'business to business' the onus rests with the individual. How should he behave when representing his company?

Respect hierarchies

Every business has its own hierarchy. Just as you have a recognised position in your company's order of seniority, so has the person you are dealing with in his own.
    You should always:

- *Make your status clear* when you meet for the first time. Use a business card as a minimum, adding helpful information about the structure that you fit into – for example, 'I look after the southern region – my boss is John Arnold, our national sales manager.'

- Establish the *other person's position* in the company structure and in particular whether he is more senior or junior to you. (Remember different firms have different titles and that a divisional manager in a multinational is likely to be much more senior than the managing director of a tiny company.)
- Use a *level of formality* appropriate to your respective positions. Thus, equals are likely to be quickly informal (for example, using first names soon after meeting) while a more junior person should always adopt the level of formality dictated by the more senior (it is bad manners for example, for a junior salesman to greet the MD of a potential customer on first meeting with a slap on the back and cheery, 'Good morning, Fred!').
- Decide on the *most effective way to exploit your respective struc-tures*. This means agreeing how decisions and communications should be handled, not only between you and him but also between your respective bosses. Most managers have had the experience of being bypassed at some time or another by a decision being taken over their heads and know that it ranks among the most unacceptable forms of behaviour, par-ticularly when it involves someone from outside the company. Getting your lines of communicatoin clear from the outset should minimise this hazard.
- *Leave* handling the complexities of *your contact's hierarchy* to him – there are no plaudits to be won from becoming embroiled in the internal politics of another business.

Among the problems you may meet in handling another organisation's hierarchy are:

- Being let down by your main contact. It is courteous to give him a fair opportunity to take corrective action before taking your complaint higher in his company; it is also sensible because the internal diagnosis is always going to be biased in their interest rather than yours.

- Changing levels of contact after an initial meeting. It is common for the first contact between businesses to be at high level (when a new account is won, for example) and subsequent business to be done at a lower level. There is no problem with this except where there is an implied promise that all contact will be at the high level. It is very discourteous to allow this impression to go unclarified.
- The other business fails to handle your hierarchy correctly. This can be very irritating but you should always put the wider interests of the relationship between the two firms ahead of any personal slight that you might feel.

Be loyal to your firm

It can be tempting to share any problems you or your firm are having with a friendly person from another organisation. You may strongly disagree with some aspects of your company's policy or find that you are asked to defend the action of a colleague who has made a foolish decision. How should you behave in these cases?

- Remember that *criticising your own firm* in front of others diminishes the image and status not only of your company but also yourself. People respect loyalty and gossips and tittle tattles may enliven the passing hour at the bar but never win sincere approval. You should reserve your criticism for the privacy of your own office or factory.
- *Defend the actions of your colleagues* – particularly when you don't have all the facts – but always acknowledge the concern of the person making the complaint. Equally, never attempt to defend the obviously indefensible – it only makes you look foolish. The best cure for valid criticism is the promise and delivery of effective and speedy corrective action.

- Although a certain amount of gossip is a vital ingredient in most effective relationships, you should *avoid the spiteful and malicious.*

Speak well of your firm

If you are to be a good ambassador for your firm you should always be well briefed about what is going on in it. It is embarrassing to be told by a third party something about your company that you should have known yourself. Accentuate positive aspects of your firm's activities and be ready to talk about its success stories even though they might not directly affect your part of the organisation. Showing pride in your firm is infectious and it is good manners to brief yourself on the achievements of the firms you deal with to avoid sounding too much like a one-sided commercial.

Handling the pressures when your firm has publicly known problems can be difficult. The trick is to be diplomatic without being pompous. Speak honestly but discreetly, and remember that you don't have to answer every question that you're asked.

Handling complaints

Complaints may be made orally or in writing and may be:

- Addressed to you personally
- Addressed to your boss or some other senior person
- About something that is, or is not, your fault.

How should they be handled?
The ground rules are very simple:

- Complaints should always be *immediately and politely acknowledged* by the recipient (however outrageous the complaint may seem) and either the problem sorted out or the intended follow-up action and timetable indicated (for example, 'I shall take up your complaint with the despatch department and respond further within five working days').

- Any individual criticised should be *told immediately and fully* of the complaint and should always be given the benefit of any doubt involved.
- Complaints should be examined from the *standpoint of the customer* and explanations or remedial action should always respect this.
- Responses to complaints should always be *courteous, firm and complete* (or clear as to what remains outstanding to be done). Never hide behind the façade of the firm by using words such as 'We, at International Consolidated, have always adopted the policy, etc . . .' or 'In the considered opinion of the writer, etc . . .' but write in personal and simple terms as though you were offering the explanation across the desk to a respected colleague. Remember that it is the tone of the explanation or the apology which is as important as its substance.
- When the circumstances warrant, *say you're sorry* – don't hide behind facile explanations or smallprint get-outs. Organisations can be judged on how they handle complaints and it's no coincidence that this aspect forms an important part of BS5750 or IS9000 accreditation.

You may be on the receiving end of a totally unreasonable complaint that makes you very angry. Try this tip. Get the anger off your chest by writing a letter that says it all – but don't post it. Read through it after a couple of days, tear it up and *then* write the more measured response that does you and your company credit.

The negotiation minefield

Many business-to-business dealings are to do with negotiating – buyer to seller, client to adviser, company to banker, and so on. Everyone involved understands the objective – to reach a mutually satisfactory conclusion after a process of controlled disagreement. Understanding the rules of the process and the etiquette that participants are expected to observe is a vital aspect of success. Many negotiations founder because one party unwittingly sabotages the process through naivety or ill manners. What follows are some 'dos and don'ts' to help you steer a path through the negotiation minefield.

Do

- *Make your own proposition clear* (even though it will be understood not to be your final position). Much time is wasted and irritation caused by one party having to tease out what it is that the other is looking for.
- *Make the best of your case.* There is no need to draw attention to its weaknesses – leave that to the other side.
- *Be prepared to respond* when the other party concedes a point, but your concession doesn't need to match his.
- *Be courteous, polite and thoughtful* without acting weakly. Tantrums and aggressive posturing seldom impress serious and experienced negotiators.
- *Be prepared to compromise to reach a conclusion.* The great majority of negotiations can be concluded in one meeting and the deal made on this basis usually proves more durable than one involving long and arduous haggling. Of course, you must be clear in your own mind at the outset the minimum terms which are acceptable to you if this approach is to work.

Don't

- *Tell lies.* There is a clear distinction between a subjective claim ('we have the best product on the market') and an objective claim ('we have outsold every other manufacturer in the first quarter of this year'). The latter must always be capable of independent verification whereas the former is a matter of opinion.
- *Spring surprises* by, for example, introducing totally new fac-

tors at the eleventh hour unless it is done purely to gain a tactical advantage over the other party with whom some long-term relationship is not planned.

- *Be emotional, intolerant or insulting* to attempt to gain advantage over the other party – it seldom works. 'Play acting' is sometimes employed in high-level negotiations in which the parties establish their relative bargaining positions using what might best be described as 'commercial charades'. It is not recommended for the everyday round of commercial transactions.

The rules of etiquette applying to most commercial negotiations assume a degree of independence in the process. If one party clearly has the dominant role – perhaps to the extent that it can impose a deal on the other – the only thing the weaker party can do is hope that the other will act honourably. After reminding them of the above dos and don'ts of course!

Confidential material

Many negotiations involve one party giving the other confidential information which could be useful to a competitor or damaging in some other way. Confidentiality agreements, which protect the rights of the parties involved in a deal, have become more common as fewer and fewer businesses are willing to rely on the integrity of the people they deal with. Successful long-term business relationships are still largely based on mutual trust, and a demonstrated ability to respect confidences, over and above the strict legal requirements of a confidentiality agreement, forms an essential part of this.

Here are some guidelines to help you handle confidential material:

- Always keep confidential material in *as few hands as possible*. Work on a 'need to know' basis and remind everyone of the importance of security.
- Keep *records secure* and use *code names* where the identity of

the parties needs to be protected. Take copies of key documents personally to reduce the involvement of other staff.

- Where necessary talk *off the record,* agreeing that no notes of the conversation will be kept and that confidences exchanged will be wholly respected.
- Respect *any reasonable conditions* placed by the other party on who should have information provided (it is *unreasonable* to ask you to withhold information from your colleagues if it is material to the outcome of the negotiations.
- Expect *mutual observance of confidentiality* and if it appears that the other party has 'leaked', take it up with them immediately; even if they have broken your trust, resist the temptation to retaliate.

Acting honourably

You and your company will be judged by the standard of both your public and private behaviour. What constitutes honourable behaviour will vary according to the country, the time and the state of commercial and personal ethics. However, as a general rule, honourable business behaviour is *acknowledging and responding to the firm's wider responsibilities without resorting to excuses, subterfuge or deviousness.*

Companies with honourable images:

- Acknowledge problems quickly and openly
- Explain their position honestly and fairly
- Deal with third parties with generosity and compassion (within their means) while not simply relying on legal minima.

Equally, things promised in negotiations can often not be legally enforced. Honourable behaviour demands that these unenforceable promises should be complied with in full.

If businesses were people, the watchwords of honourable behaviour would be 'Let your conscience be your guide'.

A good loser

Ideally, negotiations leave both parties accepting the outcome as a reasonable solution. In some cases, however, one party becomes a loser (for example, failing to win a competitive bid or when an apparently good deal turns sour). There is no inherent merit in being a good loser if you have been misled or unfairly dealt with – there are clear legal remedies for those cases. However, the loser who cries too loudly about his self-induced misfortune only draws criticism.

To be a good loser you should:

- Apply your energies to *damage limitation in private* rather than shouting 'Foul' in public.
- *Not unfairly criticise a successful adversary.*

Handling customers and suppliers

A company's good manners are seldom more evident than when it deals with the people it buys from and sells to. You can no doubt think of companies that have a good reputation for business manners and others that have bad ones. These reputations are hard won and persist over long periods of time. What makes the difference?

Prompt and fair

Most businesses act quickly and fairly when it comes to dealing with their big customers and suppliers (they would be foolish not to!). The real test is how they handle the small and financially unimportant customer or supplier. Do they receive late and inferior service? Does the small supplier have to wait longer for his money? Is the small customer's complaint put at the bottom of the in-tray?

It is not just a matter of good etiquette that businesses should expect equality of service from each other. It makes *sound economic sense* to organise business operations to deal with all customers and suppliers promptly and fairly. Computer technology providing fast and responsive services is often a source of valuable competitive advantage.

There are some important measures of whether or not you are handling this problem appropriately. They are:

- The *number of complaints* you record for each group of suppliers or customers
- The extent of *customer loyalty* measured by repeat business
- The willingness of your suppliers to *meet your emergency needs*.

If all three are negative, you almost certainly have a problem!

The benefit of the doubt

There are often circumstances in which someone's word has to be trusted in the absence of a written record (for example, a supplier might have acted on a telephone call from his customer for which no record was made). Many businesses protect their position by adopting the attitude, 'We'll accept it only if you can prove it' and in consequence irrevocably lose the goodwill of the people they deal with.

Clearly, businesses cannot afford to be a soft touch for any claim made on them, and managers always have to be aware of their responsibilities to their shareholders. However, there is a clear role in the etiquette of business for wise judgements based on giving the third party the benefit of the doubt.

In practice, businesses should:

- *Never adopt an adversarial approach to matters in doubt until it is clear that a major difference exists*
- *Refer* matters in which the company can exercise discretion *to a sufficiently high management level* for the overall impact of the issue on the business to be judged

- *Concede* matters of doubt, however poorly supported, when the effect on the business is *trivial in the context of the relationship involved.*

Recognising mutual interest

Many businesses treat their relationships with suppliers as being of a temporary nature and equally distrust their customer's loyalty to them. As a result, each transaction is handled in a more adversarial way than perhaps is in the longer-term interest of either party. Negotiations are handled on the basis of winning the best possible immediate result, often at the expense of corporate goodwill. In many countries, including Germany and Japan, it is commonplace for suppliers and customers to collaborate in long-term activities underpinned by a degree of security largely unknown in the UK. Much can usefully be learnt from their example.

Mutual interest usually rests on a common understanding of shared goals. The customer may want security of supply at competitive prices; the supplier needs the assurance of a reliable customer to justify investing in plant and research and development. To initiate a discussion based on mutual interest you should:

- Establish the willingness of both parties to *share longer-term plans*
- Agree how *confidential material* is to be handled
- Agree the *main parameters* of the commercial relationship (for example, qualities, quantities, price reference points, and so on)
- Decide on a *divorce clause* to allow either party to withdraw if things don't work out.

Like most aspects of the etiquette of one business dealing with another, identifying and acting in mutual interest is based on trust, integrity and fair trading. Competitive pressures often tempt companies to compromise their standards for the sake of a short-term advantage. They should remember that hard-won, good reputations are very quickly and easily lost!

Assess your company's performance

Does your company have a well-earned reputation for integrity and good business manners? See how it scores by completing the following checklist and referring to the answers on page 106. Always = 5, Sometimes = 3, Never = 1.

Always Sometimes Never

1. My company makes a point of putting business behaviour high on the agenda of all employees.
2. We pay appropriate respect to the hierarchies of the companies we deal with.
3. We make sure that the people we deal with understand our structure and the seniority of the people they're meeting.
4. We believe in being polite and well mannered in our dealings with all other businesses.
5. We don't act deviously in changing contact points or priorities within our structure without telling other affected businesses.
6. We don't criticise each other or our firm in front of third parties.

Always   Sometimes   Never

7. We stand up for our colleagues when they are
   criticised even though we
   may share some of the
   concerns expressed.

8. We don't gossip about each
   other to third parties.

9. We are proud of our company and speak well of it.

10. We think about and respect
    the interests of the people
    we do business with.

11. When people complain we
    handle them firmly but
    fairly.

12. When in doubt we err on
    the side of generosity rather
    than sticking to the letter of
    the law.

13. When negotiating, we
    recognise the line between
    fair play and dishonesty.

14. We avoid being emotional,
    intolerant or insulting when
    negotiating business deals.

15. We make appropriate
    arrangements to ensure that
    confidential material is kept
    secret.

16. We respect information
    given off the record.

17. We regard our word as
    being binding when given
    in a spirit of commercial
    goodwill.

Always Sometimes Never

18. We handle our customers
    and suppliers on an even-
    handed and fair basis.
19. We deal with problems
    promptly and give com-
    plainants the benefit of the
    doubt.
20. We treat business relation-
    ships as being to mutual
    long-term benefit.

Checklist scores

Add up the total score (maximum 100) and check your company's rating as follows:

75–100 Your company sets commendable standards of good
business behaviour and makes sure that everyone knows and
follows the right code. You should be glad to be working for
them.

50–75 A fairly good score but there are areas in which things
could be better. Ask yourself whether you could contribute
positively to making an improvement.

20–50 Your company is not among the most principled
around and there is considerable scope for doing better. If all
the scores are low, perhaps you should consider whether or
not this is the place for you.

CHAPTER 9
Case Studies

These case studies describe difficult situations in which someone's command of good manners is put to the test – sometimes severely!

The disappearing boss

Simon is the northern area sales manager for a multinational company making pumps and valves. Aged 29, ambitious and hard working, he is used to operating at a senior level and in his seven years with the company has built up valuable relationships with many important customers. He and his team are based in a small office in Leeds, some 200 miles from his boss, Alan, the UK sales director, who works in the head office in Surrey. Simon and Alan meet fairly regularly, sometimes in Leeds and sometimes at head office, and always visit the leading northern customers together at least once a year.

Simon has been working for two years on a potential new account which offers the prospect of substantial sales for his company. A rather traditional Yorkshire engineering firm, this family business is intensely loyal to its existing suppliers and it has taken Simon much time and trouble to persuade the chief buyer to consider his company's range. At last he has achieved the breakthrough – a meeting with the managing director and two board colleagues at which a full supply proposition can be made. Simon is convinced that Alan should attend the meeting to add weight to their presentation and Alan agrees. A date is fixed for the visit to the potential customer. Alan says he will bring with him all the presentation material and Simon agrees to collect him from Leeds station in good time for the meeting.

Simon, waiting at the station, is alarmed to find that Alan isn't on the train as planned. He waits for the next one (there would still *just* be time to make their appointment) but he isn't on that one either. He rings head office to see if Alan has been taken ill or some other problem has delayed him but finds that his secretary is sick and no one else knows anything about it. He decides that he'll have to go ahead with the meeting on his own and leaves a message with the switchboard at head office to suggest to Alan, should he ring in, that he should get a taxi to join him at the customer's office. He then rings the secretary of the customer's managing director to say that his colleague has been unavoidably delayed on his journey from London but that he'll be there as arranged. Now he knows that he'll have to make the presentation without the material that Alan was going to bring with him – quite a challenge but one which he believes he can take in his stride. That is until he reaches the potential customer's office!

Despite driving at top speed he arrives five minutes late, hot, anxious and not at his best. Instead of being shown into the meeting he is asked to wait – for 20 minutes – and is then ushered into the chief buyer's office, not into the boardroom as he'd expected. Martin, the chief buyer, looking angry, asked Simon what the '****' his company thought they were doing and emphasised only too clearly what an embarrassment this whole affair had caused him. Nonplussed, Simon protests that being late for a meeting is hardly a crime and that there had probably been a problem with Alan's train. 'Then how do you explain *this*!' storms Martin, giving Simon a fax from Alan.

Addressed to Jim Groves, the purchasing director of another of Alan's customers, it has obviously been sent to the company by mistake. Simon reads, with increasing alarm:

Dear Jim,

I've just flown in from Brussels (it's 10pm, by the way, and I've called in the office on my way home) and found your urgent message about the component problem. I'm supposed to be at a boring presentation in the north of England tomorrow with some second-division company I've never heard of but I'll come and see you instead, since we've obviously got to sort this one out pdq. I'll get Jenny, my secretary, to ring Simon, my colleague, in Leeds in the morning to give my excuses and handle the meeting alone. I've left her this fax to send you first thing in the morning and I'll be with you around 10 o'clock if that's OK.

Regards,

Alan.

Clearly, someone in Alan's office had seen a fax number on his desk and assumed it was Jim's – with disastrous results. Simon mumbles apologies to Martin who says, rather shortly, that he has work to get on with. Simon is shown back into reception. What is he to do?

He realises that his company has caused offence to Martin, the managing director of the potential customer and his board colleagues. He also realises that his personal standing has been damaged by something over which he had no control. He feels angry and let down.

He decides to do the following:

- He handwrites a personal letter of apology, there and then, to the managing director expressing regret at the incident and assuring him that his colleague meant no discourtesy by the comments he made in the fax. He recognises that they may have gravely impaired their chances of doing business but seeks another opportunity for he and Alan to set the record straight.

- Back in the office he writes a personal letter to Martin with apologies and regret at the embarrassment he has caused and asking whether they may still keep in touch – perhaps meeting for lunch at some early date.
- He does not tell his staff what happened but explains that the meeting had to be cancelled at the last minute.
- He writes a personal note, in appropriately strong terms, to Alan telling him of the unwelcome problem he had to cope with and the offer he has made by letter to the managing director, and asking him to ring him directly to give his renewed apologies.

Is there anything more Simon could have done? Probably not. It might have been tempting to 'cut and run' or pour the blame on the inefficiencies and arrogance of his head office. Neither would have given the potential customer any feeling of the regret which Simon's company quite properly should have felt about this small, but important, error of judgement.

The Arab deal

Alex is the PA to Sir James, the chairman of a leading company with a wide circle of friends and contacts among senior business people. Alex has worked for him for some years and, although he is not always the easiest boss, they get on well and she prides herself on her quiet efficiency. Their relationship is still quite formal (he refers to her as 'Miss Jenkinson') but Alex knows that he relies heavily on her tact and understanding.

The office is in a quiet backwater of the West End of London and it provides the perfect venue for the discreet meetings which are so much a part of Sir James's business life. He handles some very confidential and secret negotiations – take-overs, large contracts, liaison with politicians and the like – and his current preoccupation is signing a large contract with a Middle Eastern government. All the technical work has been done, tenders submitted and accepted and credentials checked. All that remains is the signature of the contracts by the relevant Minister during a visit to London.

Alex's preparations for the visit are meticulous – everything is planned from the flowers in the suite at the Dorchester to making sure that the boardroom will be swept for bugs on the morning of the meeting. Nothing can go wrong – or can it?

The meeting is arranged for 11am and a limousine is arranged to collect the Minister at 10.45am. Sir James will be attending a meeting in the City but will be back by 10.30am in good time to greet his guest.

At 9.30am Alex is startled to be told by reception that the two Arab gentlemen have arrived for the meeting. They introduce themselves, the Minister and his assistant, and explain that they had enjoyed the walk from the hotel. Alex shows them to the boardroom, offers them refreshments and rushes back to her desk to tell Sir James that their guests have arrived. He suggests she makes sure they have everything they need and promises to be back as soon as he can.

Returning to the boardroom the guests don't seem troubled by the delay but ask Alex for an extra copy of the contract so that they can spend the time checking over some of the details. Eager to keep her guests happy she readily complies.

At 10.20am Sir James returns and goes straight to the boardroom and, moments later, arrives at Alex's desk asking where the visitors are. 'They're probably in the loo' is Alex's first thought but reception soon confirm that the visitors have 'just stepped out to buy a small gift for their host'. They don't come back. At 11am the limousine arrives bringing the real Minister and his assistant. Both Sir James and Alex are devastated.

What are the issues for good business manners?

- It was essential that the meeting was kept secret but someone found out about it. Who was it and how did they do it? It could be a competitor, a rival Middle Eastern politician or a commercial spy. The leak could have occurred in London or in the Arab state concerned. The question for Sir James and Alex to answer is whether *they* did everything they could to ensure the secrecy of the meeting.

- Was Alex correct in not questioning the credentials of the visitors? Checking the identity of senior people is a sensitive matter and she was probably right to take them at their word. However, she was wrong to give them a copy of the contract without being *absolutely certain* who they were. She should have explained, perhaps, that only Sir James had copies of the documents and that they would have to await his return.

- What more could Alex have done? She could have cancelled the limousine and perhaps learnt from the Dorchester that the guests were still in the hotel. She can't reasonably be criticised for either lapse.

- What should Sir James do as a matter of good business manners? First, he must tell the Minister of the morning's events and promise a full enquiry into them. He should offer apologies (even though his company may not have been at fault) and suggest that his guests might need time to decide whether or not they wish to continue with signing the contract as arranged. Beyond that he can only pray for a successful outcome!

The meeting muggers

Jonathan has been a member of his company's quality management committee for some years. It performs an important function in the firm, bringing together managers from all the main disciplines to find ways to improve both products and procedures. The chairman of the committee reports directly to the managing director and everyone in the company knows that it is a job which carries a lot of clout. As production planner, Jonathan has always had an important contribution to make to the work of the committee and he is delighted to be told that he is to take over the chairmanship.

He prepares carefully for the first meeting, reviewing minutes, making sure that the agenda contains all the relevant items, that everyone is available and that any paperwork to be discussed on the day has been circulated. The meeting goes well, discussion is open and constructive and a number of useful actions agreed on. Until, that is 'any other business'.

Darren, the design manager, asks Jonathan to explain to the meeting what exactly are the powers of the committee. Jonathan has never seen a written constitution for the committee (it was formed long before he joined it) and the best he can do is to say that the powers were established by custom and practice and that everyone knows that the managing director pays a lot of attention to what it says. Darren, with the support of several others, claims that the committee must have a proper mandate from the company and agreed working procedures if its members are not to waste their time. After discussion, Jonathan volunteers to discuss this with the managing director and report back.

The MD is not very sympathetic, 'We all know what the committee does – it's worked well for years – why do we need to bog it down with bureaucracy?' However, he says that if Jonathan would feel better with a rule book he should go ahead and write one.

Using the Works Council as a precedent, Jonathan draws up a set of rules which are duly adopted at the next meeting. And then he finds that the previously informal and constructive meetings become slow, formal and divisive. Resolutions are formally tabled, amendments moved, votes cast, chairman's prerogatives challenged and the rule book constantly invoked. To Jonathan it becomes a nightmare. He realises that the committee has been ambushed by Darren and two of his colleagues with the result that its work has become a joke. He has a heated meeting with Darren but fails to persuade him to go back to the old methods. He suspects that someone in the company wants the quality management committee 'sterilised', but who is it?

Jonathan fears that he will soon lose the job of chairman of the committee if he doesn't act – but what should he do?

- His first obligation is to think of the good of the company. He is convinced that a strong committee does useful work and believes the MD will support action taken to achieve this. However, he owes a duty both to the company and to his fellow committee members, however much he may disagree with them.
- His first action should therefore be to express his concerns openly and fully to his committee with a clear recommendation that they abandon the new constitution. He should not threaten resignation but indicate that he will have to take other action if he is not supported. He must also keep his own boss, the production director, fully informed on a strictly confidential basis.
- If the committee is adamant that it wishes to go on as before, his next action should be to discuss the situation with the MD (expecting, not unsurprisingly, to hear the words, 'I told you so') with a request to take whatever action is needed to restore the original harmonious working of the committee. Jonathan must know that he puts his chairmanship on the line at this point and that the MD might well replace him with someone else.
- Given the backing of the MD, Jonathan should then formally suspend the new rules at the next meeting and, dealing with each person individually, remove the troublemakers from the committee. He should make sure that his boss is in the picture at all stages because he can anticipate criticism from the departmental heads of the managers he removes. At the next meeting he should inform the remaining members, and any new appointees, of his action and resume normal business thereafter.
- Reflecting on the episode, Jonathan would be well advised to recall the old maxim, 'If it ain't broke, don't fix it!' Efficient

business practices don't rely on form and procedure but on team spirit and effective leadership. Both were put in jeopardy by the meeting muggers!

Further Reading from Kogan Page

Customer Care, Sara Cook
Customer Service, Malcolm Peel
Effective Meeting Skills, Marion E Haynes
How to Communicate Effectively, Bert Decker
How to Speak and Write Persuasively, Robert Vicar
Managing Cultural Diversity at Work, June Jackson and Khizar Humayun Ansari
Readymade Business Letters that Get Results, 2nd edition, Jim Douglas
Report Writing in Business, Trevor J Bentley